monday morning™

BODYART:
WORLD HOLIDAYS

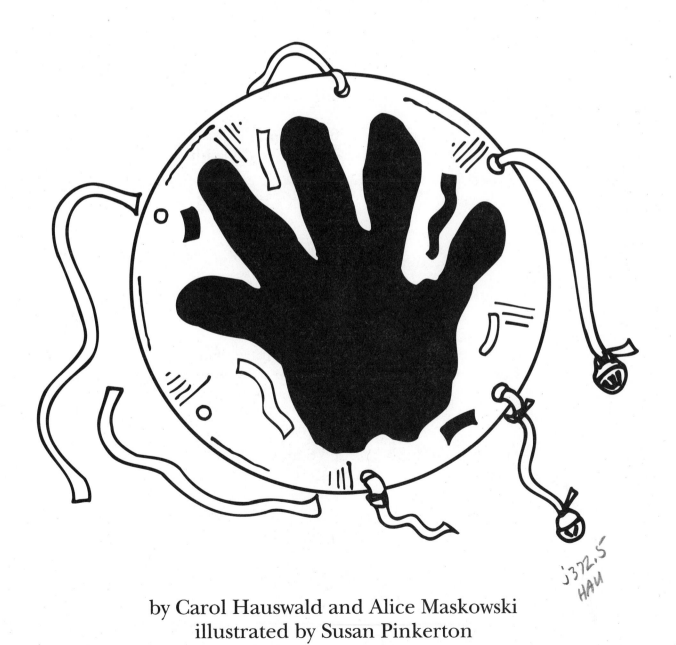

by Carol Hauswald and Alice Maskowski
illustrated by Susan Pinkerton

In memory of Bobbie,
who taught us the pioneer spirit

Publisher: Roberta Suid
Editor: Carol Whiteley
Design & Production: Susan Pinkerton
Cover Art: David Hale

On-line address: MMBooks@AOL.com

P.O. Box 1680, Palo Alto, CA 94302

1-878279–94-7
Printed in the United States of America
987654321

CONTENTS

INTRODUCTION

A good luck dragon made from an egg carton and the paper outline of a child's foot. A panda made from the outline of a child's hands and a plastic milk bottle. A clothespin Christmas angel whose wings are the replicas of a child's hands.

The pages that follow provide models and simple directions that will enable you and your children to produce these and scores of other special-day creations based on hands, fingers, feet, toes, and other body parts. You'll also find related bulletin boards, crafts, songs, action verses, games, and snacks that turn *BodyArt* into a whole-learning environment that fosters imagination and self-esteem.

Celebrating Celebrations

This multi-sensory approach to learning focuses on seven special-day units:

China's Feast of the Lanterns. Teng Chieh, one of the oldest holidays, has been celebrated for more than 2,000 years; it is part of Chinese New Year festivities. *BodyArt* projects, ranging from exciting fireworks to good luck dragons to "hand-some" lanterns to gentle-looking pandas, are part of this wonderful day.

A European Christmas. Old World English, French, and German Christmas traditions come alive in this *BodyArt* section. A "Twelve Hands of Christmas" bulletin board acts as a game. Additional festive activities enable children to create mistletoe crowns, candles, chalets, and clothespin angels.

India's Holi and Basanta. Spring festivals Holi and Basanta are happy occasions and a favorite time for Indian children. Your children will enjoy the special related projects that *BodyArt* provides, from creating a bulletin board map and Indian elephant to a Bengal tiger and snow-capped mountains.

Ireland's Saint Patrick's Day. Everybody's Irish on Saint Patrick's Day—or at least that's what we all say every March 17! Children will love the shy little leprechauns that are part of the *BodyArt* bulletin board, as well as the silly shamrocks and smiling spuds.

Israel's Birthday. One of the youngest as well as the oldest countries celebrates its birthday on May 14 every year. To commemorate this special occasion, bands play, flags wave, and girls and boys rejoice by dancing. *BodyArt* offers children a variety of activities, from making stamps and stars to creating flags and flowers.

Mexico's Dias de los Muertos. While Mexico's "Days of the Dead" takes place around Halloween, it's not a scary time. Families remember those who have passed on, and share many happy memories. *BodyArt* joins in the festivities with a hanging *novio,* or heart, as well as sun and cloud flowers and a traveling suitcase.

United Nations Day. A little known holiday, but one that is important to the fostering of world peace, United Nations Day is celebrated each year on October 24. During this learning unit, children are introduced to the worldwide peacekeeping organization through activities that are designed to increase global awareness.

Literature Links

Each unit of *BodyArt: World Holidays* includes a list of picture book read-alouds. These books will awaken and sustain children's interest in language and in the subject matter covered. The books are sensitively written, beautifully illustrated, and age-appropriate; they make wonderful springboards to the units. Many of the read-alouds also tie directly to specific *BodyArt* projects. For example, Brian Wildsmith's *The Twelve Days of Christmas* makes a good introduction to the European Christmas bulletin board, appropriately named "The Twelve Hands of Christmas."

The picture books may also be used as follow-ups to *BodyArt* activities. The stories will inspire creative drama, puppetry, spontaneous games, child-drawn picture books, movement songs, child-dictated stories, and more—activities that all contribute to whole-language learning.

All of the read-alouds listed are readily available through libraries and bookstores. Inexpensive paperback editions can often be purchased through children's book clubs. Two clubs that we use frequently are:

The Trumpet Club
666 Fifth Avenue
New York, NY 10103

Scholastic, Inc.
730 Broadway
New York, NY 10003

Another good source for books is:
Sundance Distributors and
   Publishers
P. O. Box 1326, Newton Road
Littleton, MA 01460

Materials for the *BodyArt* Projects

The projects in this book require common arts and crafts supplies that most preschool centers have on hand: nontoxic tempera or finger paints, crayons, washable markers, nontoxic glue, scissors, hole punches, poster board, construction paper, paper fasteners, and rolls of colored bulletin board paper. *Note:* When using tempera paint, mix with a small amount of Staflo starch. This makes the paint adhere better to paper, and eliminates flaking; it also gives a nice sheen to the finish. You can make your own finger paint by using a 50-50 mixture of tempera paint and starch. This will cut down on your material costs substantially.

Whenever possible, we recommend the use of recycled materials—items such as paper towel rolls, egg cartons, plastic milk bottles, cardboard from cereal boxes, and wallpaper samples. Using recycled supplies will keep student projects inexpensive—and make them earth-friendly too!

Where Do You Go from *BodyArt: World Holidays*?

If you and your children enjoy the projects in this *BodyArt* book, you may also be interested in the five other books in the series that employ this creative approach to learning. *BodyArt: Seasonal Holidays* covers Sukkot, Passover, Easter, April Fool's Day, Kwanzaa, New Year's Day, and Children's Day. *BodyArt: Holidays U.S.A.* celebrates the earth, Native American tribes, children, American leaders, explorers, and animals. *BodyArt: People* explores families, feelings, friends, and community. *BodyArt: Nature* features four-legged animals, birds, fish, insects, spiders, and seasons. And *BodyArt: Holidays* celebrates Halloween and harvest time, Hanukkah and Christmas, and "I Love You Days." Together these body-based arts and crafts books form a solid curriculum with which you can involve your children in enjoyable learning all year long.

What Is BodyArt?

Like all activities that build self-esteem, *BodyArt* begins with the children. *BodyArt* projects are arts and crafts activities based on the young creator's hands, fingers, feet, toes, and other body parts. The outlines and shapes of these body parts are then enhanced with a wide variety of free or inexpensive crafts materials and transformed into special works of art.

But *BodyArt* projects are much more than simply coloring within the lines or filling in worksheets. Intricately woven into them are children's own imaginations and personal perceptions. When viewing a circle, adults see the shape; but a child who has just drawn a circle may see a hot air balloon, an iridescent bubble, or a turtle with its head and feet pulled in. *BodyArt* draws on young children's creativity, and allows children to make unique contributions to their own projects—because without their special bodies and minds, there would be no artwork. Final products, therefore, will be treasured for years as testaments to the children's talents and uniqueness.

The projects themselves are fun and easy to do. Colors are bright and brash, lines are big and bold, shapes are repeated over and over again. As the children work through the activities, they become involved in a magical world, one that's bursting with excitement and meaningful involvement and learning.

One of these types of learning is preparatory learning. The child learns how to cut with scissors, which is a prewriting skill. He or she also learns how to make marks on paper, which fosters eye-hand coordination.

Academic learning also takes place with *BodyArt* units. After a unit is completed, for example, children have a better notion about measurements and directions. Finally, each *BodyArt* unit is designed to be sensitive to the needs of gender, culture, and ecological considerations. And all *BodyArt* learning is child-friendly.

Activities are slanted toward children from preschool to grade 1. At the earliest developmental level, children will simply provide the necessary body part for tracing and cutting by the adult; they'll complete the project by decorating the shape. More advanced children can trace the shapes themselves and assist in the cutting, as well as decorate. Older children will be able to handle all the tasks on their own. But no matter how much of a project young artists do, their efforts will lead to increased confidence. Each "I did it" experience will motivate children to achieve at ever-higher levels of learning.

In a nutshell, *BodyArt:*

• uses language for real, meaningful purposes so that children are able to make sense of their world and their place in it;

• actively involves children through experiential, inductive, and democratic processes;

• recognizes the learning environment as a social community in which educational resources are found;

• incorporates a wide variety of tactile, kinesthetic, visual, and listening activities that reach all learning styles;

• is highly adaptable to the typical learner, as well as to gifted and talented and learning-challenged children.

CHINA'S FEAST OF THE LANTERNS (TENG CHIEH)

Teng Chieh, the Feast of the Lanterns, is a holiday that's more than 2,000 years old. And its birthplace, China, is one of the world's oldest civilizations.

The celebration, held in the evening, begins with a great parade; everyone pours into the streets holding lanterns. A huge dragon leads the parade, and as the parade moves along, strings of firecrackers are set off. The noise the firecrackers make is reputed to be louder than the fireworks at an American Fourth of July display!

While Teng Chieh marks the end of the 15-day New Year's celebration in China, it's a good way to begin the New Year with your children. They're certain to remember the fun they have making the *BodyArt* firecracker bulletin board, lantern, dragon, and panda.

Fireworks Bulletin Board

Fireworks are usually associated with the celebration of Independence Day in the United States. But fireworks were first used during festivals and religious ceremonies in China a thousand years ago, just after the Chinese invented gunpowder. Fireworks are still used in China's New Year's celebration.

Materials: Nontoxic, washable red tempera paint; shallow Styrofoam tray; 16" x 20" piece of white tagboard

Directions: To make the fireworks display, ask each child to take a turn dipping the palm of one hand into a pan of red tempera paint. Keep the paint undiluted so that it will not run. Next, have the children press their palms (one at a time) to the white tagboard. Show them how to start in the center of the board and spiral outward until the board is filled with large rings of red handprints. Add sticky dots in a variety of colors to make the fireworks even more fun!

Note: For two fireworks displays, start the spiraling rings midway down the sides of the tagboard and at least five or six inches toward the center. This will leave enough room to "fan" the handprints out.

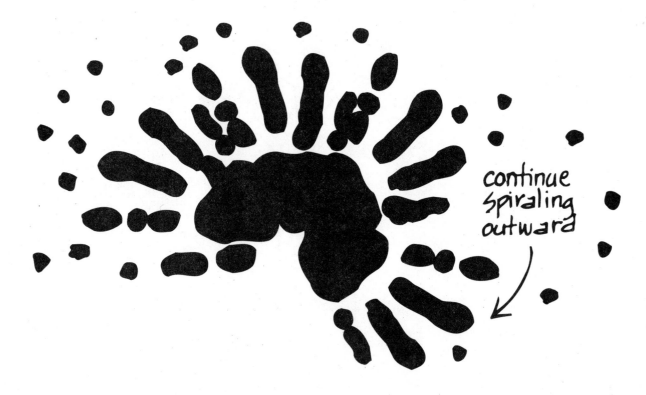

continue spiraling outward

"Hand-some" Lanterns

Lanterns are believed to bring good luck in China. Many lanterns are painted red because the color red means joy and life to the Chinese people!

Materials: 8 1/2" x 11" piece of red construction paper; nontoxic, washable yellow tempera paint; shallow Styrofoam tray; scissors; transparent tape

Directions: To make their own three-dimensional lantern, children dip one palm into a shallow tray of yellow paint. They then make yellow imprints over the entire surface of their sheet of red construction paper. When the paper is completely dry, help the children fold it in half vertically. Then cut one-inch slits across the folded paper. Stop cutting about two inches from the edge. Have the children fold their papers width-wise and tape the ends together. Cut out, bend, and tape a 1" x 8" paper handle to the top of each lantern so each child can easily carry the New Year's creation.

Note: Encourage children to make two imprints from each "dip" into the tray. This will speed up the drying process (which usually takes about an hour). It will also help keep the paint from caking and make the paper easier to cut when dry.

fold and cut

bend and tape

tape

Good Luck Dragons

In China, the dragon is the symbol of goodness and strength. It also stands for happiness and good luck. Usually the decorative dragon is made of bamboo and covered with silk or paper.

Materials: Green nontoxic, washable paint; brushes; pencils or markers; green construction paper; wiggly eyes; cardboard egg cartons; red crepe paper; scissors; white fabric paint; staplers and staples; cardboard tubes; nontoxic glue; transparent tape

Directions: Begin by painting one entire egg carton and one cardboard tube with green tempera. While the materials are drying, ask the child to trace his or her foot on green construction paper. This will be the dragon's head. Cut out the paper foot and glue a wiggly eye on each side of the heel. Then paint on shiny white teeth with fabric paint on both sides of the front of the foot, starting with the middle toe and working your way back to the mid-section.

To add color and make the dragon "breath fire," staple an 8" piece of red crepe paper to the dragon's mouth. Then staple two joined 8" strips of crepe paper to the rear portion of the egg carton for a tail.

The green-painted cardboard tube will be the dragon's neck. Simply fit it over one of the egg carton dividers; it will stay in place and still be able to move and turn. To make the tube more secure, roll up a small piece of transparent tape and press it to the inside of the tube before fitting the tube over the divider.

To attach the dragon's head to its neck, cut a half-inch slit on either side of the top edge of the cardboard tube. Slide the head into place, and have a roaring good time!

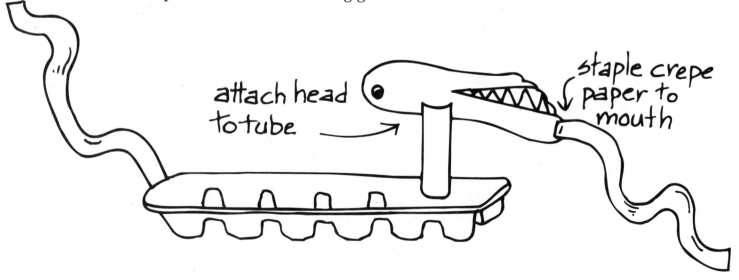

attach head to tube

staple crepe paper to mouth

Panda Keepers

The panda is so well-liked throughout the world, especially by children, that it is the symbol of the World Wildlife Fund. Not only do *BodyArt* pandas hold crayons and art supplies, but they also help children appreciate the need to take care of endangered species. For more information, write to the World Wildlife Fund at 1255 23rd St. NW, Washington, DC 20037.

Materials: Gallon-size plastic milk bottle, panda head reproducible (p. 16), black construction paper, scissors, wooden craft stick, non-toxic glue, transparent tape, lightweight cardboard or tagboard, white chalk, pencil or marker

Directions: To make the panda, copy and cut out the panda reproducible and glue it to a piece of cardboard or tagboard. Cut out the board to the shape of the head. Then tape a craft stick to the back of the head, leaving most of the stick extending down below the head.

Next, cut a half-inch slit in the top portion of the plastic milk bottle. The panda head will be slipped into this slit. Then cut away the back of the milk bottle, making sure you leave enough of the sides so that hands can be taped on. Cut across the back of the panda body four inches up from the bottle's bottom. When cutting is complete, the pour spout and surrounding square should be separate from the rest of the milk bottle.

To make panda arms and feet, trace the child's hands (closed in a fist) and feet onto black construction paper with white chalk and cut out. Glue or tape the hand cutouts to either side of the panda's body. Glue the paper feet to the bottom of the milk bottle, making sure the toes stick out.

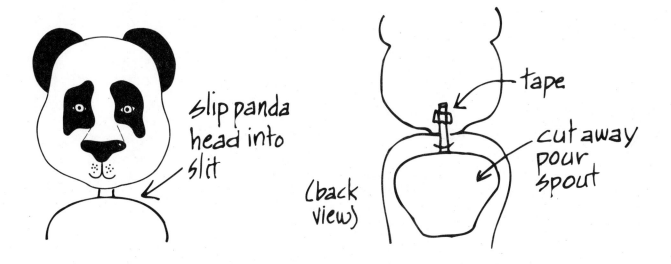

slip panda head into slit

(back view)

tape

cut away pour spout

Feast of the Lanterns Finger Plays and Movement Songs

My Little Lantern
(to the tune of "The Farmer in the Dell")

My lantern shines at night,
My lantern shines at night,
Heigh-ho the derry-o,
My lantern shines at night.

It shines on a big parade,
It shines on a big parade,
Heigh-ho the derry-o,
It shines on a big parade.

My lantern sees a dragon,
My lantern sees a dragon,
Heigh-ho the derry-o,
My lantern sees a dragon.

The dragon waves hello,
The dragon waves hello,
Heigh-ho the derry-o,
The dragon waves hello.

My lantern waves goodbye,
My lantern waves goodbye,
Heigh-ho the derry-o,
My lantern waves goodbye!

New Year's Song
(to the tune of "Here We Go 'Round the Mulberry Bush")

This is the way we see the new year,
See the new year, see the new year.
This is the way we see the new year,
Our lanterns shining bright.

The big, green dragon brings good
　luck,
Brings good luck, brings good luck.
The big, green dragon brings good
　luck,
All on New Year's Day.

Firecrackers are loud in our ears,
Loud in our ears, loud in our ears.
Firecrackers are loud in our ears,
All on New Year's Day.

When lanterns burn out we go to
　sleep,
Go to sleep, go to sleep.
When lanterns burn out we go to
　sleep,
All on New Year's Day.

Little Panda
(to the tune of "Rock-a-bye Baby")

Rock-a-bye panda, on the treetop,
Gently smiling at all those who stop.
He reaches out slow and finds some
　bamboo,
Nibbles it shyly the way pandas do.

China Read-Alouds

Fiction

Demi. *Liang and the Magic Paintbrush.* New York: Holt, 1980.

Liang wants to paint but he can't afford a paintbrush. Then he receives a magic paintbrush and his drawings come alive in this "Reading Rainbow" featured offering.

Demi. *Dragon Kites and Dragonflies—A Collection of Chinese Nursery Rhymes.* New York: Harcourt, 1986.

Charming rhymes that are ideal for young children are offered in this collection. Nicely illustrated in a large format that children love.

Garrison, Christian. *The Dream Eater.* New York: Aladdin Books, 1978.

Yukio is a little boy who has a bad dream. No one in his village wants to comfort him because the people have their own bad dreams. Fortunately a friendly *baku* helps solve the entire village's nightmare problems by simply gobbling up all the bad dreams!

Hooks, William H. *Peach Boy.* New York: Bantam, 1992.

An old Japanese man and woman are worried about who will take care of them. They find a giant peach in the river from which a boy comes out. The boy helps protect the village from the Oni monster.

Jensen, Helen Zane. *When Panda Came to Our House.* New York: Dial, 1985.

A lovely learning picture book that introduces children to the ways of the Orient—from the giant panda to the mythical phoenix. Black and white drawings by master illustrator Chris Van Allsburg.

Kent, Jack. *There's No Such Thing as a Dragon.* Racine, Wisc.: Western Publishing Co., 1975.

Billy's dragon grows bigger because his mom doesn't believe in dragons. Once she admits there is a problem, the dragon shrinks in size and becomes much more manageable.

Louie, Ai-Ling. *Yeh-Shen.* New York: Philomel, 1982.

Ed Young illustrates this Cinderella story from China. It's a wonderful story that gives a new slant on the version typically read to young children.

Mahy, Margaret. *The Seven Chinese Brothers.* New York: Scholastic, 1990.

This classic tall tale tells of seven Chinese brothers, each of whom has a very special talent. Beautifully illustrated by Jean and Mou-sien Tseng, this picture book is set in the time of Ch'in Shih Huang—the emperor credited with beginning the construction of the Great Wall.

Mosel, Arlene. *Tikki Tikki Tembo*. New York: Henry Holt, 1968.

A long, honorable name isn't an advantage when your brother can't say it fast enough to get help and rescue you. Even so, children love to memorize Tikki's name and say it when this old Chinese folktale is read aloud to them.

Seidler, Rosalie. *Panda Cake*. New York: Parents' Magazine Press, 1978.

Read this story to children and they'll find out that panda cake is very special indeed! It's made with apples, roots, bamboo shoots, and clover honey for topping.

Tullman, Marcia and Deborah DeRoo. *Mei Ling's Tiger*. Littleton, Mass.: Sundance Publishers & Distributors, 1993.

This story centers on a Chinese family living in a modern city. The little girl thinks she sees a tiger hiding here and there, but the tiger turns out to be a domestic cat.

Walker, Barbara. *The Most Beautiful Thing in the World*. New York: Scholastic, 1993.

This multicultural Big Book tells a folktale from China in which three sons are sent out to bring back the most beautiful thing in the world. The ruler/father decides the youngest son's caring heart wins the contest.

Whipple, Laura. *Eric Carle's Dragons Dragons*. New York: Philomel, 1991.

A fascinating account of all sorts of mythological creatures—from Chinese dragons to mermaids. Illustrated by Eric Carle and nicely peppered with poetry compiled by the author.

Williams, Jay. *Everyone Knows What a Dragon Looks Like*. New York: Four Winds Press, 1976.

Han is a poor orphan gate-sweeper but he is the only one who believes the old man is really the great dragon who can save the village.

Wyndham, Robert. *Chinese Mother Goose Rhymes*. New York: Philomel, 1968.

Illustrated by Ed Young, this charming collection of Mother Goose rhymes proves that children's poetry is alike in many ways—no matter what country it comes from.

Young, Ed. *Lon Po Po*. New York: Scholastic, 1989.

This Little Red Riding Hood story from China is a Caldecott Medal winner and comes from an ancient oral tradition. In this version, three sisters successfully trick the wolf.

Young, Ed. *Seven Blind Mice*. New York: Scholastic, 1992.

It's hard to identify an elephant when you're a visually challenged mouse!

Nonfiction

Olliver, Jane. *The Doubleday Children's Atlas*. New York: Doubleday, 1987.

China, India, Italy, and the United States are only a few of the countries featured in this visual account of the world's geography. Photographs and page-size maps help teach basic concepts to children.

China Snacktime

Delicious Dragons

Refrigerator breadstick dough makes a fun and easy snack for young children! Preheat your oven to 350 degrees and grease a baking sheet. Then unwind the dough—each 11 oz. tube makes 8 breadsticks—and flatten to $1/2$-inch width. After washing hands thoroughly, children can form the dough into their own dragon shapes. Place the critters on the prepared baking sheet and bake for 15 minutes until lightly browned. Place the delicious dragons on a rack to cool. Serve with red jelly (dragon's fire) and peanut butter.

China Game

Dancing Lights

What Chinese lantern festival would be complete without a rousing game of dancing lights? To play, all you need is a flashlight or penlight and lots of imagination! Turn the light on and wiggle it slowly on the floor. Ask the children to try to follow the dancing light as it winds its way around and around the floor. Sing to the songs on p. 12 while the light is on. When you turn the light off, children can take a rest. Caution children to look where they are going to avoid collisions!

A EUROPEAN CHRISTMAS
(GREAT BRITAIN, FRANCE, GERMANY)

Old World traditions that have been passed down from one generation to the next come alive when celebrating Christmas in countries such as England, France, and Germany. The *BodyArt* activities associated with these celebrations focus on the different ways European countries celebrate this important holiday. They also help children appreciate other aspects of the Christmas season in addition to gift giving.

In this unit, children will become involved in such projects as creating angels, chalets, candleholders, mistletoe, and, of course, a Christmas tree. As you begin, we offer you and the children a greeting from a traditional English carol: "We wish you a merry Christmas!"

Twelve Hands of Christmas Bulletin Board

Bring European charm and tradition to your classroom with this interactive bulletin board. The board also serves as an interactive learning game!

Materials: Green construction paper, scissors, poster board, transparent tape, Twelve Days of Christmas reproducibles (pp. 27-28), crayons or markers

Directions: Trace 12 hands (fingers apart) onto green construction paper. Cut out the paper hands and arrange on a large poster board in four rows with fingers pointing down; the hands will form a pyramid-shaped tree. When the hands are positioned, tape the heels to the board with transparent tape; the "hinge" will allow the paper fingers to be lifted. Beneath each hand, tape the appropriate colored reproducible. Children will look forward to seeing which picture is hiding under a "bough" each day! They can also learn to count from 1 to 12.

Option: Add stickers, paper ornaments, or pictures of fruit cut from magazines to the tree.

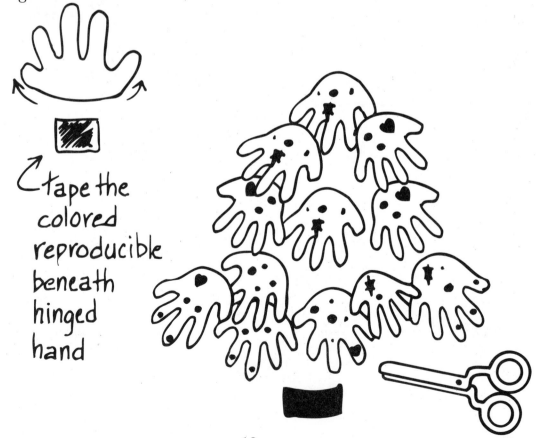

tape the colored reproducible beneath hinged hand

Merry Mistletoe Crowns

In ancient Britain, the mistletoe was the sacred plant of the Druids. The widespread appearance of this parasitic plant is attributed to the mistle thrush, a bird very fond of holly berries. Because of its evergreen leaves, mistletoe represents endurance and hope. Mistletoe is still draped today inside homes and over doorways to bring good fortune.

Materials: Large paper plate; scissors; pencil or marker; red nontoxic, washable paint; green construction paper; nontoxic glue; shallow paint tray

Directions: Cut a hole in the center of the paper plate, large enough to fit on the child's head; the remaining paper band should measure approximately 1 1/2" wide. To make mistletoe, trace the child's hand (fingers apart) onto green construction paper seven times. Cut out the paper hands and glue the heels to the paper plate band, fingers sticking out. Ask the child to dip one finger into the red tempera paint and make holly berry imprints on the green "mistletoe" (berry prints on the paper band are fine too). Let dry completely.

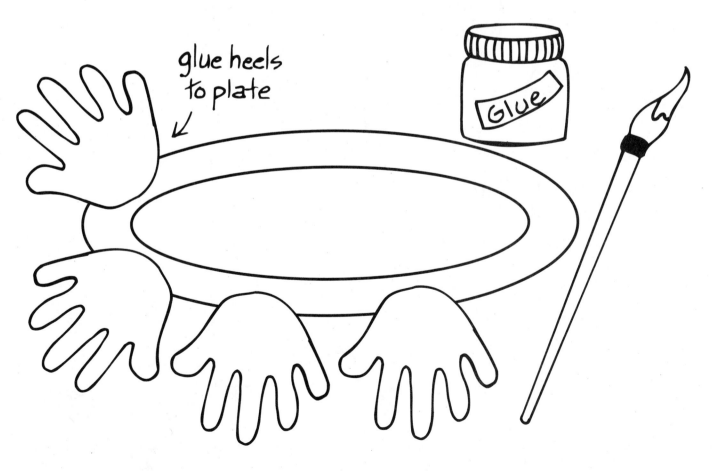

glue heels to plate

Glue

French Candles

Joyeux Noel! The holiday candle is a French symbol of hope. After making these *BodyArt* candles, children can imagine that it's the night before Christmas in long ago France.

Materials: Yellow, white, and black construction paper; nontoxic glue; scissors; transparent tape; pencil or marker

Directions: To make the candle base, trace the child's foot onto a piece of black construction paper. Cut out the paper foot. Roll the heel up and over and tape to the mid-foot area. To make the candle, cut an 8 1/2" x 11" piece of white construction paper into thirds. Roll one of the strips and tape edges for a tall cylinder. Make 1" cuts at the bottom, flatten fringe out, and glue to the black candle base. To add a flame, trace the child's hand (fingers apart) onto a piece of yellow construction paper. Cut out the paper hand and insert the heel portion into the top of the candle. Glue in place with fingers extended outward to represent flames.

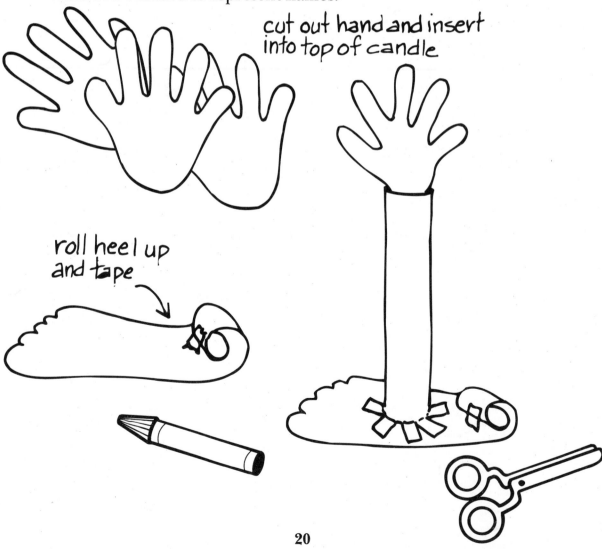

cut out hand and insert into top of candle

roll heel up and tape

20

Doll Pin Angels

Introduce this activity by reading the book *White Nineteens* by David Christiana, which tells about a tiny creature who has so many wings she has to assign them numbers! In Germany, children write letters to the Christkindl girl before Christmas to tell her whether they have been good and to list the gifts they'd like.

Materials: One doll pin and stand (available at craft stores or by writing to Forster Manufacturing Co., Inc., Wilton, MA 04294); nontoxic, washable tempera in a variety of skin-tone colors); brush; gold glitter; pipe cleaner; poster board; self-sealing plastic bag; pencil or marker; nontoxic glue; scissors

Directions: Paint the doll pin with the skin color of your choice. While it's drying, trace the child's hands (fingers together) onto poster board. Cut out the paper hands and glue the thumbs to the back of the dry doll. When the glue is dry, bend the fingers forward and back again to create a flying effect. To make a collar and halo, wrap a pipe cleaner around the neck and then up above the head of the angel (cut off excess pipe cleaner). Carefully add glue to the wings (front and back), body, and stand and sprinkle on glitter (be sure children keep glitter out of their faces and eyes). Let the angel dry completely. Place in a plastic bag for safekeeping.

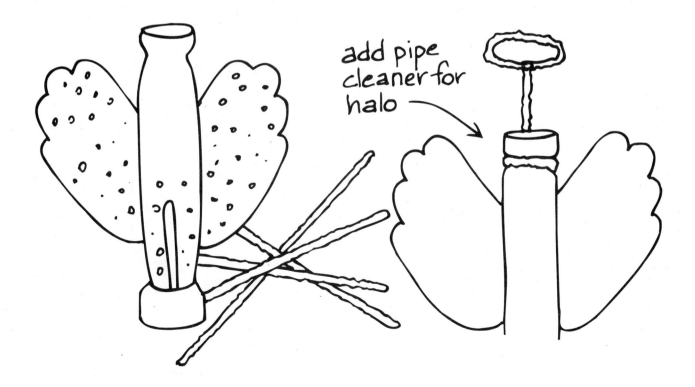

add pipe cleaner for halo

Brown Bag Chalets

Frohliche Weihnachten! In Germany, the Christmas holiday season lasts from the end of November through mid-January. Many American holiday traditions originated in Germany, including the Christmas tree and the visit by Saint Nicholas. In winter, family gatherings are held in lovely chalets with snow covering the roofs.

Materials: Brown paper lunch bag, strips of newspaper, staples and stapler, crayons, white poster board, scissors, transparent tape

Directions: Use crayons to draw a door, windows, and a windowbox garden on the front of the bag. Then gently fill the bag with strips of newspaper and close with a piece of tape. To make snow, trace the child's hand (fingers apart) onto a piece of white poster board. Repeat. Cut out both hands. Position one paper hand so that it drapes over the roof at the front of the bag (fingers pointing down). Position the other hand similarly so it covers the back of the roof. Staple the two snow hands together, then cover the staples with a small piece of transparent tape.

European Christmas Finger Plays and Movement Songs

Holiday Magic Song

(to the tune of "Oh, Do You Know the Muffin Man?")

Oh, do you know the Christmas
   angel,
The Christmas angel, the Christmas
   angel?
Oh, do you know the Christmas angel
Who comes on Christmas Day?

Oh, do you know Saint Nicholas,
Saint Nicholas, Saint Nicholas?
Oh, do you know Saint Nicholas
Who comes on Christmas Day?

(You may substitute Sinter Klaas—the
Dutch name for Saint Nicholas used
by the colonists—if you prefer.)

Merry Mistletoe Song

(to the tune of "Ten Little Indians")

One green, two green, three green
   mistletoes,
Four green, five green, six green
   mistletoes,
Seven green, eight green, nine green
   mistletoes,
Ten green mistletoes!

One red, two red, three red berries,
Four red, five red, six red berries,
Seven red, eight red, nine red berries,
Ten red holly berries!

One kiss, two kisses, three little kisses,
Four kisses, five kisses, six little kisses,
Seven kisses, eight kisses, nine little
   kisses,
Under holly berry mistletoe!

Holiday Tree Action Verse

First we find our green tree just like
   this.
(Shield eyes and look around.)
Then we take it in the house just like
   this.
(Carry heavy tree on shoulder.)
We have to make it stand up just like
   this.
(Stand tall as a tree.)
Then we decorate it prettily just like
   this.
(Hang ornaments on a tree.)
And string the lights just like this.
(Hang a string of lights.)

European Christmas Read-Alouds

Fiction

Baynton, Martin. *Jane and the Dragon.* Martinez, Calif.: Discovery Toys, 1988.

More than anything else, Jane wants to be a brave knight. Thanks to a dragon, she gets her chance. Her outwitting him saves the day!

Brett, Jan. *The Wild Christmas Reindeer.* New York: Putnam's, 1990.

Now that it is almost Christmas, it is Teeka's job to get the reindeer out on the tundra ready to fly on Christmas Eve. Nothing works until Teeka thinks of a new way to talk to them.

Christiana, David. *White Nineteens.* New York: Farrar, 1992.

This wonderfully illustrated story tells about Buttercup, who has a beautiful wing wardrobe; she has so many she has to number them. When her favorite white #19s disappear, she sets out on an exciting journey to find them.

Gaber, Susan. *The Princess and the Lord of Night.* New York: Harcourt, 1994.

There's a curse on the princess, and it takes problem-solving by readers to remove it.

Hazen, Barbara Shook. *The Knight Who Was Afraid to Fight.* New York: Dial, 1994.

This sensitive offering in cartoon form tells about a knight who can't stand blood. So he solves his problems by peaceful means.

Hodges, Margaret. *Buried Moon.* Boston: Little, Brown, 1990.

Granny tells a young girl that long ago there used to be bogs, swamps, and fever-giving marshes on the farm. People feared these great pools of black bog water, and Granny tells a story about when the moon was buried in them.

Hodges, Margaret. *Saint George and the Dragon.* Boston: Little, Brown, 1984.

When monsters and giants stalked the earth, a noble English king becomes a big hero, especially for slaying dragons.

Keats, Ezra Jack. *The Snowy Day.* New York: Penguin, 1976.

This charming classic tells about a young boy who discovers all the magic of a snowy day. A Caldecott Award Book.

Kent, Jack. *The Twelve Days of Christmas.* New York: Parents' Magazine Press, 1973.

A young girl's joy turns to dismay as larger and larger gifts arrive from her true love during the 12 days of Christmas. (The book may be used as a humorous complement to the "Twelve Hands of Christmas" bulletin board.)

Littledale, Freya. *The Snow Child*. New York: Scholastic, 1978.

This charmingly illustrated Russian folktale tells of an old man and his wife who are unhappy because they have no children. Watching children build a snowman, they decide to build themselves a snow girl-child. The snow child comes alive and provides much joy for the old couple every winter.

Maccarone, Grace. *The Sword in the Stone*. New York: Scholastic, 1992.

Aimed at younger children, this read-to tells about the famous King Arthur.

McCully, Emily Arnold. *Mirette on the High Wire*. New York: Putnam's, 1992.

Madame Gateau's boarding house on English Street shows what life was like in Paris 100 years ago.

Moore, Clement. *The Night Before Christmas*. New York: Holiday House, 1980.

Tomie de Paola's illustrations make this traditional story a real treat for young children.

Oxenbury, Helen. *The Queen and Rosie Randall*. New York: Morrow, 1979.

The queen has gotten into one of her muddles and needs Rosie Randall, a little girl, to help her solve a problem.

Pearson, Tracey Campbell. *We Wish You a Merry Christmas*. New York: Dutton, 1983.

This beloved Christmas carol from the west country of England comes alive in song and pictures that are very funny—especially those about figgy pudding!

Quin-Harking, Janet. *Magic Growing Powder*. New York: Parents' Magazine Press, 1980.

More than anything else, King Max wants to be taller. But he finds out the hard way that there are worse things in life than being short!

Small, David. *Imogene's Antlers*. New York: Crown, 1985.

Everyone sees Imogene in a new light the day antlers grow out of her head. Her mother faints, her principal glares, the birds sit and eat donuts from her antler "branches." It looks as if Imogene will have to go through life as a reindeer. Then she wakes up the next morning with a brand new challenge to see her through another exciting day.

Spier, Peter. *Christmas!* New York: Trumpet Club, 1983.

Children can use this story as a model to create their own story—or dictate one. A wordless celebration of all the activities involved in preparing for Christmas.

Van Allsburg, Chris. *The Polar Express.* Boston: Houghton Mifflin, 1985.

In his unique style, Chris Van Allsburg creates an enchanting and mysterious story in which a boy is transported to the North Pole by a very special train. A Caldecott Medal winner.

Wildsmith, Brian. *The Twelve Days of Christmas.* New York: Franklin Watts, 1972.

A lovely illustrated picture book that helps you celebrate Christmas with your children. Use this offering to launch the European Christmas unit.

Nonfiction

Aliki. *A Medieval Feast.* New York: Harper & Row, 1983.

The king is coming to visit Camdenton Manor in the year 1400. Readers learn in this charming factual account what has to be done to prepare a feast in the Middle Ages.

Cuyler, Margery. *The All Around Christmas Book.* New York: Holt, 1982.

Readers learn about the origins of various familiar Christmas rituals and how customs vary around the world. Includes instructions for making international Christmas treats and decorations, plus ideas for holiday games.

Kelley, Emily. *Christmas Around the World.* Minneapolis: Carolrhoda Books, 1986.

Here's a charming look at the December celebrations and traditions of Christians in Mexico, Iran, China, Sweden, Iraq, Spain, and Norway.

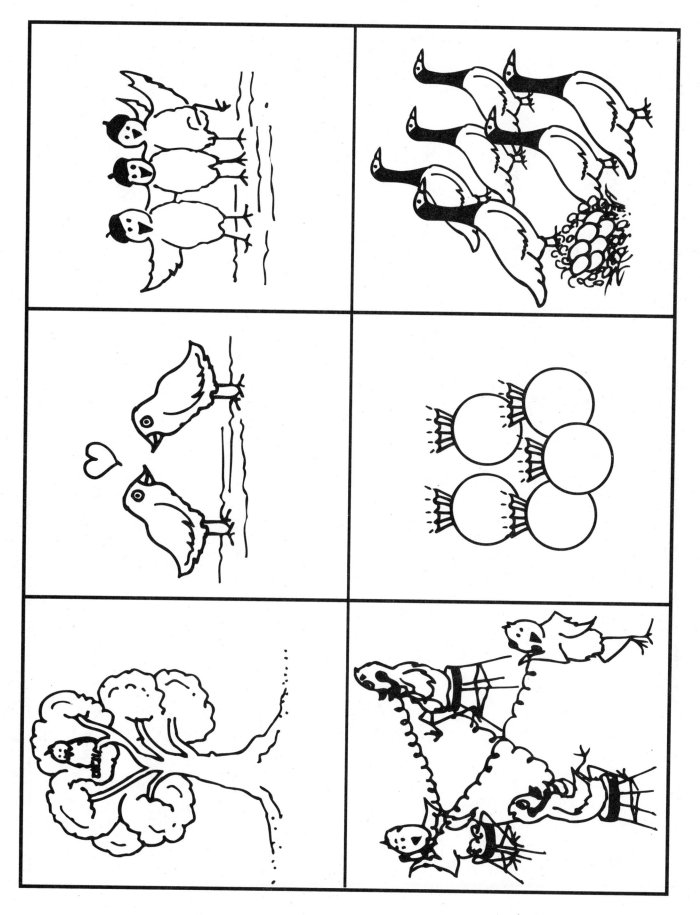

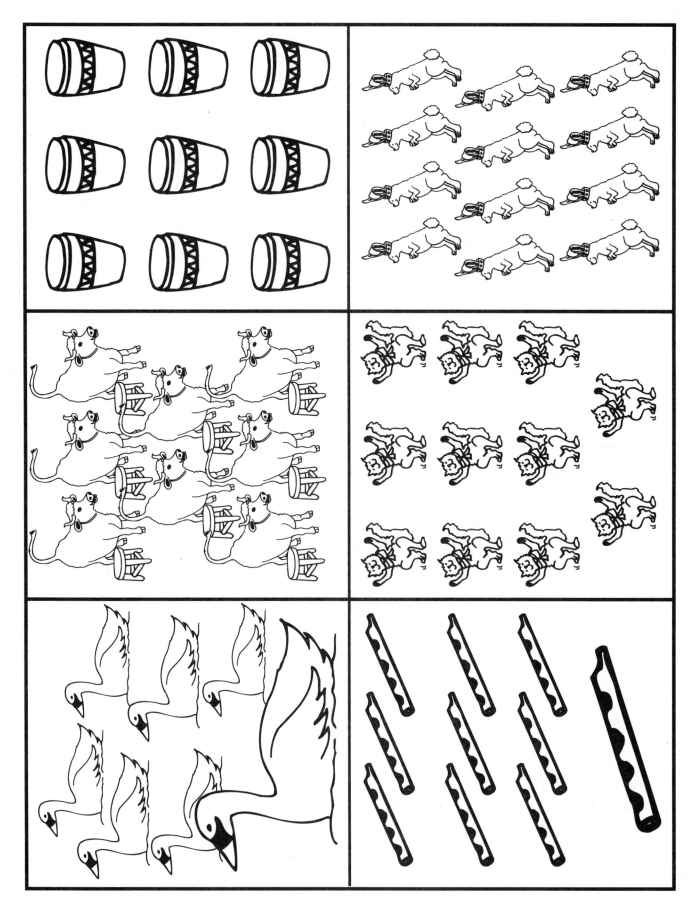

INDIA'S HOLI AND BASANTA (THE SPRING FESTIVALS)

The arrival of spring is a happy time in India and Holi, the spring-time Fire Festival, is the happiest of all the Hindu holidays. Holi occurs on the 15th day of the Light Half of the Moon, in the Hindu month of Phalguna (March). Lighting a big bonfire, blowing horns, and beating drums are three ways Holi is celebrated.

Basanta Panchami (or Basanta, for short) is celebrated about three weeks before Holi. During Basanta, young men wear yellow turbans and scarves; *basanta* means yellow in Sanskit, the sacred color of India as well as the symbol of spring. Young and old alike wear green garments during Basanti to honor the green earth.

In addition to making yellow *BodyArt* flowers, introduce your children to India's majestic mountains, Asiatic elephants, and Bengal tigers in this exciting unit.

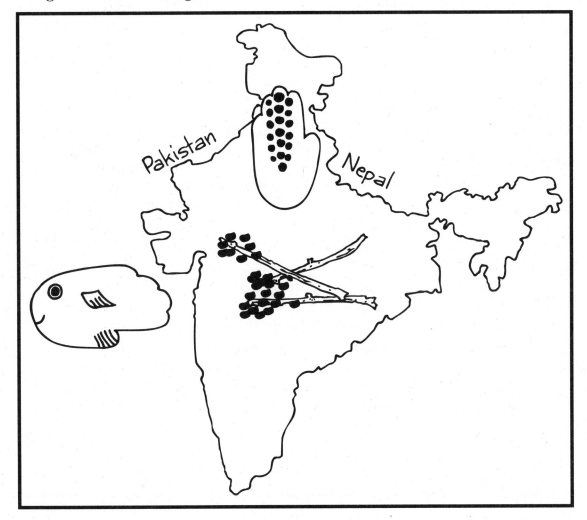

Exciting India Bulletin Board

When Christopher Columbus discovered the North American continent, he was really trying to find a shortcut to India. That is why he called the natives he found in North America "Indians." Although Columbus failed to find India, he did discover a new continent, leaving the explorer and early merchant Marco Polo to go to India to buy spices, silks, and gold for those who could afford riches in the west.

Using the reproducible map of India found at the end of this unit, teach children something about three of this country's resources by making a *BodyArt* bulletin board displaying fish, cotton, and corn.

Materials: India map reproducible (p. 38); blue poster board; tape; glue; marker; scissors; orange, green, and black construction paper; wiggly eyes; yellow and white nontoxic, washable tempera paint; twigs; shallow pans

Directions: First, enlarge the map of India either by copying the reproducible freehand or by using a copier with enlarging capabilities. Attach an enlarged copy to a large piece of blue poster board for each child. Next, make a fish shape by tracing each child's hand (in a flat, fingers-tight position) on a piece of orange construction paper. Cut out the paper hand, glue on a wiggly eye, and tape the fish to a blue ocean portion of the poster board.

Next, tape a *BodyArt* ear of corn to the north or head portion of the map. To make the corn, trace each child's hand (again in the fingers-tight position) on a piece of green construction paper. Cut out the paper hand. Then ask each child to dip his or her finger tip into yellow nontoxic, washable tempera. Have the children make dots vertically in the center section of the hand, up between the middle three fingers to represent corn.

Making *BodyArt* cotton is another easy "dip and do" activity. Collect several twigs and glue them onto a piece of dark-colored construction paper. Then ask children to dip one finger tip into nontoxic, washable white tempera paint and make clusters of white dots on the construction paper on either side and at the top of each twig. Tape the paper to the middle of the India map. (See the completed bulletin board on p. 29.)

Beautiful Blossoms

Yellow blossoms are favorite spring festival flowers in India. Children will enjoy making and observing these paper versions; the flowers can even help to provide a cool breeze on warm afternoons!

Materials: Yellow construction paper, marker, scissors, paper fasteners, wooden craft sticks, crayons, hole punch, nontoxic glue

Directions: Each blossom consists of six paper petals. To make a petal, trace each child's hand (fingers-tight position) onto a piece of yellow construction paper. Repeat five times. Cut out each paper hand, then decorate with crayons. Punch a hole in the center of the "heel" portion of each hand. Attach all six paper hands with one paper fastener. Glue a wooden craft stick to one of the paper hands so that the children can hold the blossoms. When the creations are complete, children will especially enjoy moving the paper petals around the paper fastener, counting from one to six.

Eyeing an Elephant

The elephant is the largest and strongest animal that lives on land. Indian elephants, somewhat smaller than African elephants, grow to be about 12 feet tall and weigh about six tons. The elephant's long trunk is particularly interesting. It's strong enough to pick up huge logs and yet delicate enough to pick up a peanut. Some Indian elephants live to be 150 years old.

Materials: Gray, green, and blue construction paper; scissors; wiggly eyes; sticky dots or hearts; nontoxic glue; pencil or marker

Directions: A child's hand (upside down) with fingers open makes a perfect Indian elephant! Trace the hand on a piece of gray construction paper, then cut out. The thumb portion is the elephant's trunk and the four remaining fingers are the feet. A wiggly eye glued to the upper left of the paper heel adds a whimsical touch, as do sticky dots or hearts on the elephant's body (all dressed up for the spring festival)!

Option: Hide the elephant among blades of *BodyArt* grass! Trace the child's open hand (fingers pointing upward this time) onto a piece of green construction paper. Repeat, then cut out the paper hands. Glue the *BodyArt* grass to a piece of blue construction paper, then glue the elephant on top for a mini-nature scene.

Snow-capped Majestic Mountains

India is so big it's often called a subcontinent. It's also separated from the rest of Asia by the Himalayas and other high mountain ranges. Mt. Everest in the Himalayas is the highest mountain peak in the world!

Materials: Purple and blue construction paper, marker, white fabric paint, brushes, nontoxic glue, scissors

Directions: To make majestic mountains, trace the child's hand (fingers-tight position) onto a piece of purple construction paper. Cut out the paper hand. Then add snow-capped peaks with white fabric paint (outline or fill in) on the top of the three middle fingers. When dry, glue the mountains to a piece of blue construction paper.

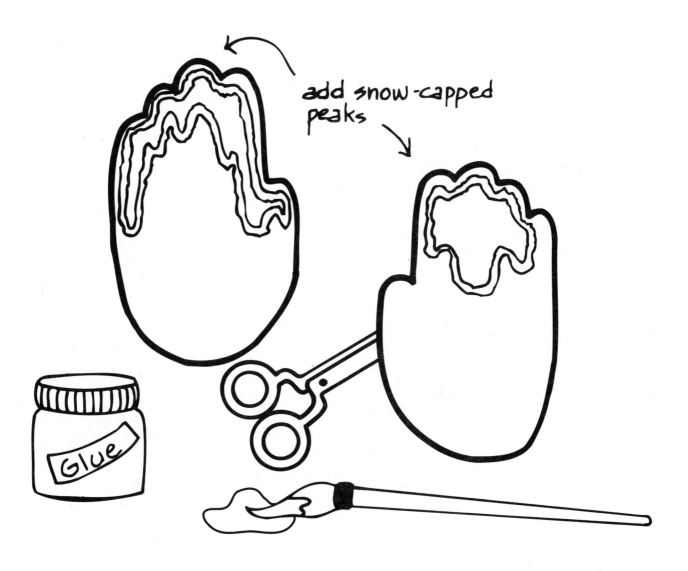

add snow-capped peaks

Bengal Tiger

This four-legged feline haunts grassy plains and jungle swamps in India. Although tigers are the biggest of all cats and are very wild and fierce, the female tiger is a devoted mother and her babies are called kittens. The Indian or Bengal tiger is yellowish tan with long, narrow black stripes all over its body and legs. An adult male weighs 400 pounds and has a tail that's nine feet long!

Materials: Tiger reproducibles (pp. 39-40), small brown paper bag, orange construction paper, black fabric paint or black crayon, scissors, nontoxic glue, orange crayons, soft scrap paper or strips of old newspaper, staples and stapler

Directions: To make each Bengal tiger, color and cut out a tiger head reproducible and glue it to the front of a brown bag. Stuff the bag with soft scrap paper or newspaper and staple shut. Color and cut out the tiger tail reproducible. Fold one-half inch and glue to the side of the bag. Next, trace each child's feet (left and right) onto a piece of orange construction paper and cut out. Decorate with black crayon or fabric paint stripes. Glue the paper feet to the bottom of the bag, making sure the toes stick out. Let the children take home their tigers for a roaring good time!

stuff bag and staple shut

fold and glue to bag

India Finger Plays and Movement Songs

The Tiger Tale

(to the tune of "Baa, Baa, Black Sheep")

Roar, roar, tiger,
Have you any food?
Yes, girls, yes, boys,
Three dishes full!
One filled with pizza,
One filled with chips,
And one filled with fruit
So I won't get sick!

Spring Colors

Yellow is the color of the bright
shining sun!
(Children form a circle with their
arms.)
Yellow is the color of flowers and
fun!
(Children pretend to hold flowers
and jump up and down.)
Green is the color of great, big
trees!
(Children stretch arms upward.)
Green is the color of my grass-
stained knees!
(Children point to their knees.)
Blue is the color of the sweet, spring
sky!
(Children hold their arms out
wide.)
Blue is the color of a bird flying by!
(Children move their arms like
wings.)

Shhh! The Elephant Sleeps!

(to the tune of "Are You Sleeping?")

Is he sleeping? Is he sleeping?
Elephant! Elephant!
My, his trunk is strong,
My, his body's long,
Run away! Run away!

He's not moving, he's not moving,
Eyes are closed! Eyes are closed!
Maybe we should sneak up,
Lift his lids and peak in,
Elephant! Elephant!

See those peanuts, see those
peanuts,
By his foot! By his foot!
He will never miss two,
One for me, one for you.
Let's be quick! Let's be quick!

One eye opens, another eye opens,
Elephant looks mad! Elephant
looks mad!
He was just pretending,
He was never sleeping,
Run away! Run away!

India Read-Alouds

Fiction

Backstein, Karen. *The Blind Men and the Elephant.* New York: Scholastic, 1992.

Blind men try to describe the way an elephant looks from their own perspective.

Birch, David. *The King's Chessboard.* New York: Dial, 1988.

Long ago in India, the king of Deccan wanted to reward a loyal servant who was also a wise man. Using a chessboard as a guide, the servant asked the king for one grain of rice on the first day for each square, double that the second day, and so on. The king granted the clever man's request, unaware of the huge amount of grain the servant was really going to get!

Bornstein, Ruth Lercher. *The Seedling Child.* San Diego, Calif.: Harcourt Brace Jovanovich, 1987.

A charming story that tells about a magic seedling child that lives inside a flower; lovely romantic pictures.

Faulkner, Keith. *The Elephant and the Rainbow.* Stamford, Conn.: Longmeadow Press, 1990.

The elephant is tired of being dull and gray. He envies all the other animals until his friends tell him they love him just the way he is.

Hirsh, Marilyn and Maya Narayan. *Leela and the Watermelon.* New York: Crown, 1971.

Leela loves watermelons until her brother decides to tease her with the tale that if you eat watermelon seeds, a watermelon will grow inside you!

Prelutsky, Jack. *The Terrible Tiger.* New York: Aladdin Books, 1970.

This tiger is so terrible (and hungry!) that he eats the village grocer, the fat baker, and the fine farmer. He meets his match when he tries to eat the old tailor.

Nonfiction

Carwardine, Mark. *The Illustrated World of Wild Animals.* New York: Simon & Schuster, 1988.

Children will love this picture book of wild animals, even if they can't read yet. The pictures will help children start learning about tigers, elephants, and other endangered animals.

Tegwill, Tony. *A Family in India.* Minneapolis, Minn.: Lerner, 1985.

In this true story, children meet Sakina, a young girl who lives with her family in Takukibowli, a village in northern India.

India Snacktime

Let the children pretend cow's milk is tiger's milk, and drink it after a rousing game of "Tigers and Elephants" (below). Accompany the milk with "Elephant Ears" from the bakery (sometimes called "Palmiers"), or bake your own.

Elephant Ears
(makes 4 pastries)

1/4 cup margarine
1 cup all-purpose flour
2 tablespoons sugar
1/2 teaspoon baking powder
1/2 teaspoon salt
1/3 cup milk
sugar
cinnamon

1. Preheat the oven to 425 degrees. Grease a cookie sheet.
2. Melt the margarine in a saucepan and set aside.
3. In a large bowl, mix together the flour, 2 tablespoons of sugar, the baking power, and the salt. Stir in the milk and 3 tablespoons of the melted margarine. The mixture should have the consistency of dough.
4. Knead the dough a few times and pat down into a rectangle on a lightly floured surface. Brush with melted margarine and sprinkle on the sugar/cinnamon mixture in a spiral shape.
5. Roll up the rectangle, beginning with a short side. Pinch to seal. Cut into 4 equal pieces. Place on the prepared cookie sheet and pat into 6-inch circles.
6. Bake the goodies for 8 to 10 minutes, or until golden brown.

India Game

Tigers and Elephants

The chase is on in this tiger and elephant game! To play, divide the children into an equal number of tigers and elephants. Then select three or four safety spots in a large playing area where tigers can hide and not be captured. After elephants chase tigers, switch roles and have tigers chase elephants.

Elephants can keep the same safety spots where they can hide and not be captured.

To avoid pushing or tackling, players make captures by placing a small, light hankie on the captured child's shoulder. Before play begins, go over the rules clearly with the children so they know that roughness is not allowed.

Pakistan

Nepal

INDIA

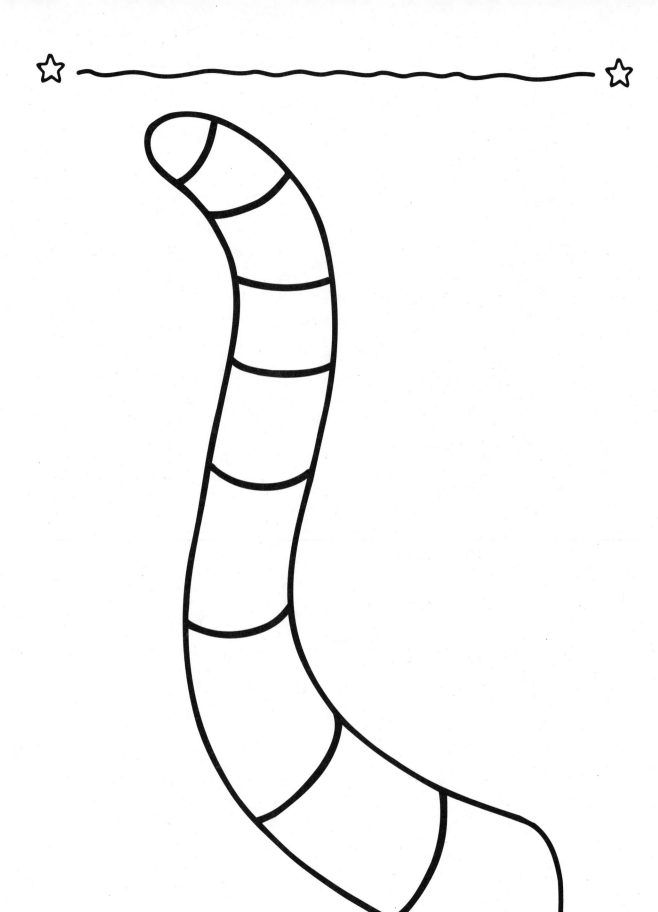

IRELAND'S SAINT PATRICK'S DAY

Young children love to learn about colors, especially if they are wearing them! Saint Patrick's Day offers an excellent opportunity to teach the color green because, as they say, everybody's Irish on March 17. Saint Patrick's Day is also a good time to learn about rainbows—where a pot of gold can be found at the end.

Children may wonder why everyone wears green on Saint Patrick's Day. It's because the green shamrock is the symbol of Ireland. And yes, there really was a Saint Patrick. He was born in Scotland around the year 387. When he was 16 years old, pirates captured him, but he went on to live a very adventurous life. The most famous story about Saint Patrick is the one in which he drove all the snakes out of Ireland. Those who doubt the story challenge skeptics to find a snake in the Emerald Isle!

Though there are no snakes in the following pages, there are plenty of rainbows, leprechauns, and, of course, Irish luck to share with the children!

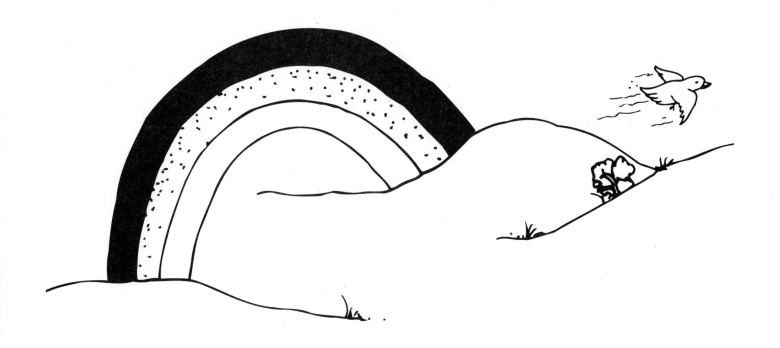

Follow Me to the Lucky Leprechaun Bulletin Board

Legend says that if you catch a leprechaun he must give you his pot of gold. It isn't easy to make him do this though. Leprechauns are wee little folk who run very fast. But even if they don't catch a leprechaun your children will see some on this bulletin board—with a pot of gold hidden beneath!

Materials: Leprechaun reproducibiles (pp. 49-50), crayons or markers (including gold), tape, glue, scissors, poster - or tagboard, construction paper

Directions: Copy and cut out four each of the lucky leprechaun face and hat reproducibles. Color with crayons or markers. Glue a hat to the top of each head. Then tape two leprechauns with hats on each side of a large piece of poster or tag board. Use a tape "hinge" so that each leprechaun can be flipped up. (See the "Where's the Pot of Gold?" game on p. 48, in which a pot of gold is hidden behind one of the leprechauns.)

Next, trace each child's foot on construction paper (your choice of colors), cut out the paper feet, and tape to the board in a random design. Post the board for all to see, and for everyone to discover the hidden pots of gold. When you've finished celebrating the Ireland unit, let the children take home their lucky paper feet!

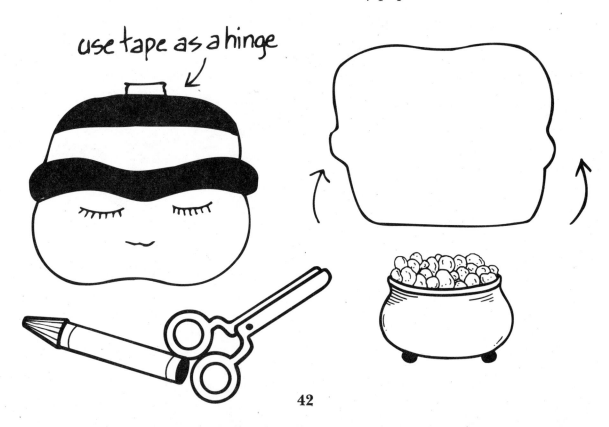

use tape as a hinge

Rainbow Hand Feather

Here's a fun way to introduce a rainbow of colors to children! This project also doubles as a feather that can be added to this unit's bulletin board.

Materials: Nontoxic crayons or washable markers in red, orange, yellow, green, blue, and purple; white construction paper; scissors; nontoxic glue or transparent tape

Directions: Trace the child's hand (fingers apart) onto a piece of white construction paper. To duplicate the rainbow color order, color the fingers according to this formula: thumb—red, index finger—orange, middle finger—yellow, ring finger—green, pinky finger—blue, palm—purple. (Optional: Make bands of colors in an arc on the paper palm, working backward from purple.) When the coloring is complete, cut out the paper hand and tape the Rainbow Hand Feather to a hat on the Lucky Leprechaun Bulletin Board.

Silly Shamrocks

Shamrock literally means "three-leaved." The shamrock's value is legendary because wearing one is the only way to frustrate a leprechaun that's teasing you!

Materials: Green construction paper; wiggly eyes; scissors; wooden craft stick; nontoxic glue; nontoxic, washable marker

Directions: Trace the child's hand (fingers tight together) onto a piece of green construction paper. Repeat two more times. Then cut out the paper hands and overlap their palms with fingers extending outward. One hand should point north, one west, and one east. Glue the palms together in this position. Add wiggly eyes, a silly nose, and a mouth. Then glue a wooden craft stick to the back to make a puppet.

Smiling Spuds!

Here's a fun activity that ties in to the wonderful song "When Irish Eyes Are Smiling." The eyes in this case are potato eyes!

Materials: Wiggly eyes, brown or tan construction paper, scissors, brown paper lunch bag, nontoxic glue, marker

Directions: Trace the child's foot onto a piece of brown or tan construction paper. Cut out the paper foot and round out the toe area so that a smooth arc is formed. Add wiggly eyes, a cute nose, and a mouth. Glue the paper foot to a paper lunch bag. At snack-time serve spuds—potato chips, shoestring potatoes, or baked potatoes—in the bag. Protect against grease stains by putting food in a separate bag before placing it inside the Smiling Spud bag.

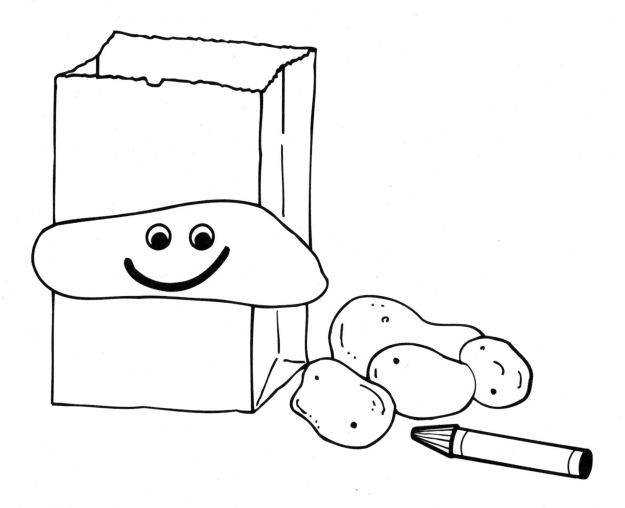

Ireland Finger Plays and Movement Songs

Wee Folk

(to the tune of "Mary Had a Little Lamb")

Patrick had a little pot,
Little pot, little pot.
Patrick had a little pot
Filled with lots of gold.

He brought the pot to work one
    day,
Work one day, work one day.
He brought the pot to work one
    day,
Which was not wise to do!

A little man saw Patrick's gold,
Patrick's gold, Patrick's gold.
A little man saw Patrick's gold
From his hiding place.

Then he cried a million tears,
Million tears, million tears.
Then he cried a million tears
That ran into the sea.

And Patrick felt so bad for him,
Bad for him, bad for him.
Patrick felt so bad for him
He gave him all the gold!

The wee man smiled and laughed
    out loud,
Laughed out loud, laughed out
    loud.
The wee man smiled and laughed
    out loud
And granted Patrick's every wish!

Shamrock Song

(to the tune of "Did You Ever See a Lassie?")

Did you ever hear a shamrock, a
    shamrock, a shamrock?
Did you ever hear a shamrock tell a
    joke?

Did you ever taste a shamrock, a
    shamrock, a shamrock?
Did you ever taste a shamrock on a
    hamburger bun?

Did you ever see a shamrock, a
    shamrock, a shamrock?
Did you ever see a shamrock dance
    all night?

Did you ever touch a shamrock, a
    shamrock, a shamrock?
Did you ever touch a shamrock on
    its tummy?

Did you ever smell a shamrock, a
    shamrock, a shamrock?
Did you ever smell a shamrock's
    basketball shoes?

Ireland Read-Alouds

Fiction

Bunting, Eve. *St. Patrick's Day in the Morning*. New York: Ticknor and Fields, 1980.

A young boy wants to be in the St. Patrick's Day parade, but everyone thinks he's too young to climb Acorn Hill. The boy proves he's old enough to have his own parade. The Jan Brett illustrations are a treasure.

Hodges, Margaret. *St. Patrick and the Peddler*. New York: Orchard, 1993.

The beauty of the Irish countryside is evident in this tale of a young boy, a peddler, and St. Patrick, who appears in a dream.

Kroll, Steven. *Mary McLean and the St. Patrick's Day Parade*. New York: Scholastic, 1991.

A beautifully illustrated tale about life in Ireland in the 1850s. The potato crop fails and the McLean family must leave their little thatched hut in Donegal and set sail for America.

Latimer, Jim. *The Irish Piper*. New York: Scribner's, 1991.

This read-to story features delightful illustrations by John O'Brien. The book tells all about the Pied Piper, who lives in the west of Ireland. Children from the town of Hamelin disappear when the town refuses to pay the piper after he rids the town of pesky rats.

Shute, Linda. *Clever Tom and the Leprechaun*. New York: Scholastic, 1988.

Tom sees a tiny man and realizes it's a leprechaun! All Tom has to do to get the leprechaun's gold is to catch him. But he finds out that's not easy!

Sierra, Judy. *The Legend of Knockmany*. New York: Scholastic, 1993.

In this Big Book multicultural tale, one giant is afraid to fight another!

Nonfiction

de Paola, Tomie. *Patrick, Patron Saint of Ireland*. New York: Holiday House, 1992.

The story of the life of St. Patrick is vividly told; perfect for young children.

de Paola, Tomie. *Tom*. New York: Putnam's, 1993.

Tommy and his Irish grandfather Tom share a special relationship in this wonderfully illustrated offering.

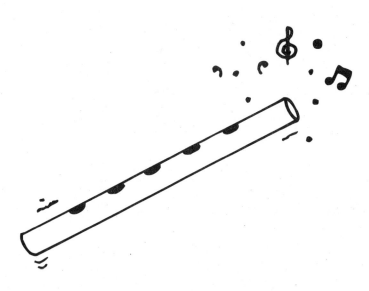

Ireland Snacktime

Green Day!

Make green jello for snacktime and serve with green fruits and veggies that children bring in to celebrate Saint Patrick's Day. Celery, green apples, lettuce, green peppers, kiwis, and green beans are all healthy snacks that children should be encouraged to eat.

Option: Add a veggie dip for fun, nutritious scooping.

Ireland Game

Where's the Pot of Gold?

To play this game, hide a colored copy of the pot of gold reproducible (p. 50) behind one of the leprechauns on the interactive bulletin board (see p. 42). Children guess where the pot of gold is. If you add clues that teach direction (left, right, over, under), this will truly be a learning game. Change the hiding place each day to make the game last longer.

"to the left and under"

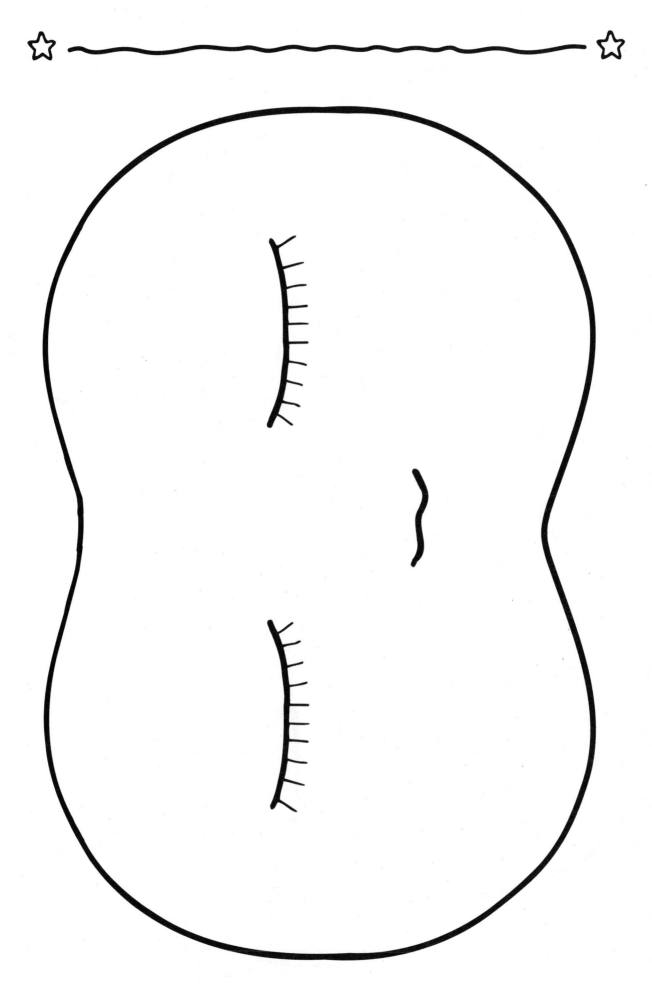

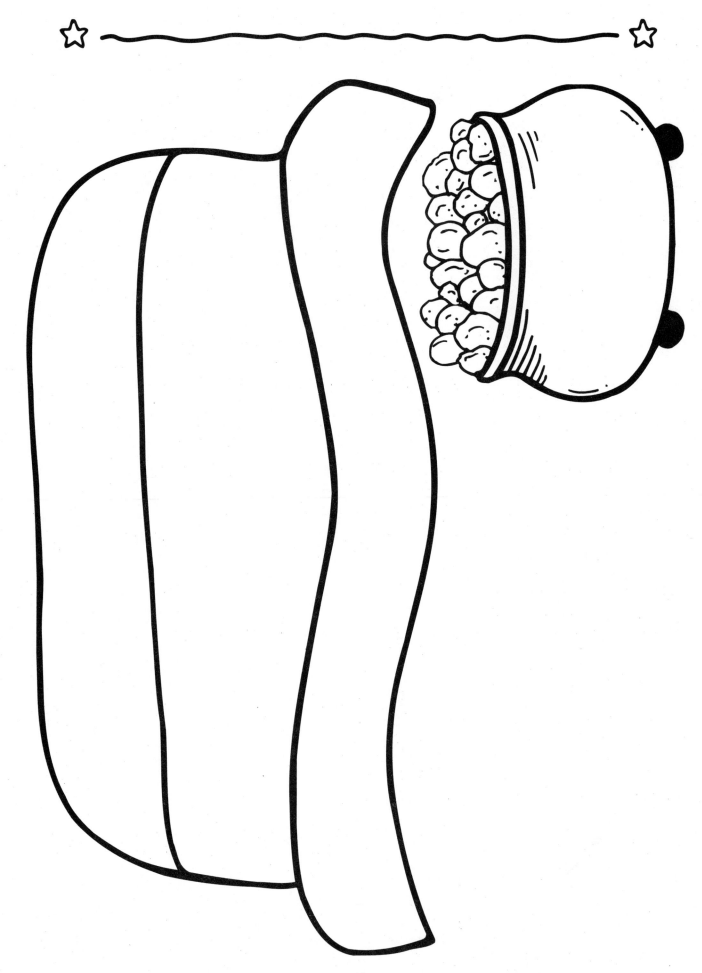

ISRAEL'S BIRTHDAY

On May 14, one of the oldest as well as the youngest nations celebrates its birthday. That country is Israel, located along the Mediterranean in the Middle East. While the area, earlier known as Palestine, was an important region since Biblical times, the modern state of Israel was actually born in 1948. In accordance with a United Nations' resolution, Great Britain withdrew its forces from Palestine on May 14 of that year, and the Jewish people proclaimed the independent state of Israel. Every year on that day, bands play, flags wave, and girls and boys dance the *hora* as they celebrate Israel's special birthday.

BodyArt lets you and your children join in on this very special occasion by creating stamps, stars, flags, and flowers—all designed to appeal to children everywhere.

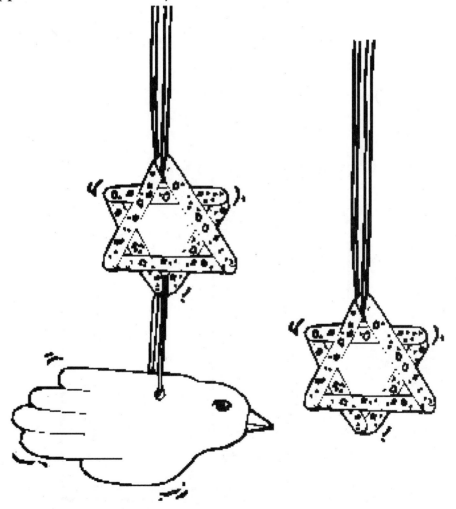

Israel's Happy Birthday
Bulletin Board

People aren't the only ones who have birthdays. So do countries!
This bulletin board celebrates the happy occasion when Israel
became an independent nation in 1948.

Materials: Glue; tape; blue crepe paper; large piece of white poster
board; shallow tray of nontoxic, washable yellow tempera; birthday-
type accessories (confetti, paper hats, glitter, etc.)

Directions: Glue four strips of blue crepe paper in the center of the
poster board. Place the strips three inches from the bottom of the
board and two inches from each other. These represent birthday
candles.

Next, ask children to take turns dipping the palm and fingers of
one hand into a tray of nontoxic, washable yellow tempera and press
their hands at the top of the "candles." There should be one "flame"
per candle.

Choose several celebration-type materials and glue or tape them
to either side of the candles. This colorful board will be a festive
focal point for a fabulous unit.

Fifty Years of Freedom
Postage Stamp

Get ready to celebrate 50 years of freedom with this special *BodyArt* postage stamp!

Materials: Reproducible postage stamp (p. 60), blue construction paper, gold crayon or glitter, nontoxic glue, scissors, pencil or marker

Directions: Trace each child's hand (fingers open) onto a piece of blue construction paper. Cut out the paper hand. Then use gold crayon or glitter to write Israel's birth year, 1948, on the paper palm. On the thumb and four fingers, write the following decades, again with gold crayon or glitter: 1958, 1968, 1978, 1988, and 1998 (you can use the abbreviations '58, '68, etc., if space is tight). Make a copy of the reproducible stamp and glue the paper hand to the center.

Floral Centerpiece

Flowers are so abundant in Israel that most of them are exported to other countries. But others are found in the wild or in home gardens, and flower vendors sell sweet-smelling bouquets in the Tel Aviv markets. This *BodyArt* flower centerpiece will be a focal point for many special occasions.

Materials: Glitter, nontoxic glue, 2 1/2" paper baking cups in a variety of colors, scissors, construction paper (in the colors of your choice, plus green), wooden craft sticks, tape or stapler, pencil or marker

Directions: Trace each child's hand onto five different colors of construction paper; the fingers may be open or closed. Cut out the paper hands. Attach a 2" x 4" strip of green construction paper to each flower for a stem. Then brace the stems by gluing a craft stick to the back of each one. Glue a paper baking cup to the center of each flower.

Cut out a 2"-high-by-18"-long strip of construction paper for the centerpiece base. Decorate one side with glitter, then glue individual flowers by their stem to the inside of the strip. Tape, glue, or staple the strip ends together to form a circle.

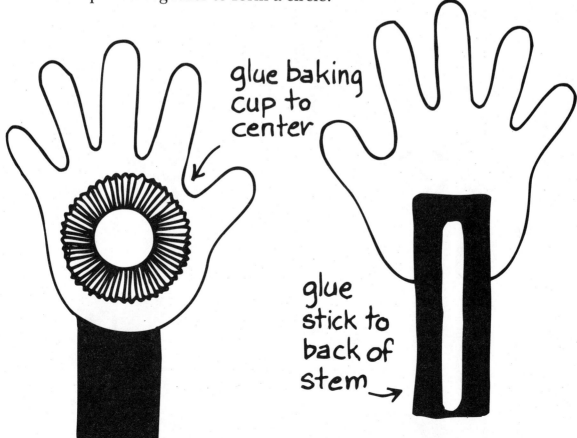

glue baking cup to center

glue stick to back of stem →

Star of David Peace Hanger

The peace-loving attributes of the dove combine with the Star of David, the traditional Jewish symbol, in this three-dimensional project that can be used during the holidays.

Materials: Wooden craft sticks (six per project), glitter, nontoxic glue, pencil, white construction paper, yarn or string, scissors, blue marker, hole punch, self-sealing plastic bag

Directions: Use a pencil to trace each child's hand (fingers closed) onto a piece of white construction paper. Erase the line that indicates the heel portion and add a circle for the dove's head. Next, outline the head and body in blue marker and add an eye to each side. Cut out the paper dove. Then punch a hole in the top center "wing" and pull an 8" piece of yarn through the hole to tie later to the Star of David.

Glue three wooden sticks together in the shape of a triangle. Repeat for a second triangle. When dry, glue the triangles together so that one is pointing north and the other is pointing south. Cover the Star of David with glue and glitter and let dry. (Encourage the children to keep their hands away from their eyes when working with glitter and to wash hands when finished.)

Slip a 6" length of yarn through the top triangle hole and knot. The yarn will enable the project to be hung on a wall or window at home. Then slip the yarn attached to the dove through the bottom triangle hole in the Star of David and knot. Cut off any leftover yarn. Place the peace hanger in a self-sealing plastic bag for the child to take home.

add circle
✓ for head

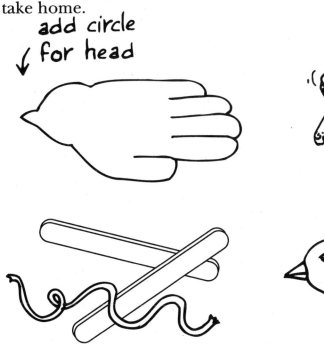

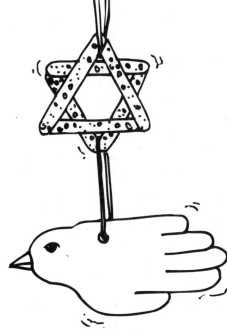

Shalom Salt Dough Paperweight

Shalom stands for peace, and this paperweight will be a daily reminder that peace is important to all people and all nations—not only at holiday times, but all year long.

Materials: Salt dough (see recipe below); wooden craft sticks; non-toxic, washable blue and white tempera paint; brushes; self-sealing plastic bags; plastic disposable garden gloves; waxed paper; self-adhesive labels

Directions: This project takes several days to dry, so adjust schedules so that children can make and shape the dough on day one, turn the paperweights to dry the bottoms on day three, and return to painting the projects on day four or five.

Begin the activity by making the salt dough and giving each child an equal portion. Place the dough in self-sealing plastic bags to allow the children to practice kneading it less messily. Salt dough will sting if it touches an open cut or wound, so have disposable garden gloves on hand for children who need them.

Pat the piece of dough out on a piece of waxed paper until it is a bit bigger than a child's hand. Ask the child to gently place one hand (fingers tight together) on top of the dough. An adult or older child can cut around the child's hand using a blunt wooden craft stick. Remaining dough can be put into a plastic bag for additional paperweight projects.

Using a wooden craft stick, write the word "Shalom" in the center of the dough hand. Tag the waxed paper with a self-adhesive label showing the child's name. Put the paperweight in an out-of-reach sunny area; turn on day three so the bottom can dry. When thoroughly dry, coat the entire paperweight top and bottom with white tempera. When that dries, brush blue tempera into the valleys of the "Shalom" lettering. When the entire paperweight has dried, let the child take it home.

Salt Dough Recipe (makes approximately three paperweights)

Mix together:
1 cup salt
1 1/2 to 2 cups all-purpose
    flour
water to moisten

Gradually add:
1 cup all-purpose flour
1 cup cornmeal
1/2 cup salt
water to moisten

Shape into a ball.

Israel Finger Plays and Movement Songs

Birthday Song

(to the tune of "London Bridge Is Falling Down")

Happy birthday, Israel,
Israel, Israel!
Happy birthday, Israel,
Have a happy year!

Shalom to you, Israel,
Israel, Israel!
Shalom to you, Israel,
Peace to you!

Laugh and sing, Israel,
Israel, Israel!
Laugh and sing, Israel,
Laugh and sing!

Dance and shout, Israel,
Israel, Israel!
Dance and shout, Israel,
It's your birthday!

The Together Song

(to the tune of "The More We Get Together")

The more we learn of people,
Of people, of people,
The more we learn of people
The kinder we are.

The more we learn of families,
Of families, of families,
The more we learn of families
The sweeter we are.

The more we learn of children,
Of children, of children,
The more we learn of children
The happier we are.

Parade Game Song

(to the tune of "Here We Go 'Round the Mulberry Bush")

Here we go 'round and raise our
    flags,
Raise our flags, raise our flags.
Here we go 'round and raise our
    flags,
Our Israeli flags.

Blue and white are colors we show,
Colors we show, colors we show.
Blue and white are colors we show,
On our Israeli flags.

Star of David in the center,
In the center, in the center.
Star of David in the center
Of our Israeli flags.

Israel Read-Alouds

Fiction

Gilman, Phoebe. *Something from Nothing.* New York: Scholastic, 1992.

Now available in soft cover, this beautifully illustrated story tells of a Jewish grandfather who makes a blanket for his baby grandson. In time, the blanket wears out, but instead of throwing it away Grandpa makes a jacket out of it. Grandpa continues to make smaller and smaller items to wear until the reader thinks a lost button is the last of it. But the grown-up grandson finds yet another way to make something wonderful from the original gift.

Kimmel, Eric. *Hershel & the Hanukkah Goblins.* New York: Holiday House, 1985.

Hershel becomes a hero when he tricks the goblins and saves the village.

Kline, Carol. *Sadie, Remember.* Littleton, Mass.: Sundance, 1992.

A book dedicated to the author's Jewish grandmother Jennie and to other immigrants who left their homes for America. Charming pictures by Arthur Polonsky capture the mood and style of times past.

McDermott, Beverly Brodsky. *The Golem—a Jewish Legend.* Philadelphia: J.B. Lippincott, 1976.

This Jewish legend tells how Rabbi Lev used magic spells to create Golem.

Speregen, Devra and Shirley Newberger. *Arielle and the Hanukkah Surprise.* New York: Scholastic, 1992.

A realistic fiction offering that tells how Hanukkah is celebrated in a modern Jewish family. The surprise is that the young girl in the story is celebrating her birthday along with Hanukkah.

Zolotow, Charlotte. *My Grandson Lew.* New York: Harper & Row, 1974.

Lewis misses his grandpa, even though the boy was only two years old when his grandpa died. This sensitive story touches on a very real issue for young children. Pictures by William Pene du Bois.

Nonfiction

Adler, David. *A Picture Book of Jewish Holidays.* New York: Holiday House, 1981.

More than 13 Jewish holidays are included in this beautifully illustrated offering.

Feinstein, Steve. *Israel in Pictures.* Minneapolis, Minn.: Lerner Publications, 1988.

When Israel became a state in 1948, the new nation opened its doors to Jewish immigrants from around the world. This nonfiction account of what happened during that time is interesting, but may need to be put into simpler language for young children.

Pinney, Roy. *Young Israel.* New York: Dodd, Mead, 1963.

Children of Israel at work and at play are included in this nonfiction book. (Your local library may have copies if the book is not available in bookstores.)

Israel Snacktime

Honey Grahams

Since Israel was known as the "land of milk and honey," snacktime naturally centers around that theme. Milk and honey graham crackers are delicious reminders of the learning that is taking place during this special *BodyArt* unit.

Israel Game

Parade Game

Hold a Happy Birthday Parade for Israel! Let children join in the fun by waving flags they make by coloring and cutting out copies of the reproducible flag of Israel found on page 60. Tape a ruler to the back of each flag and play records, tapes, or CDs of Israeli music to add to the parade festivities.

Let the children know that Israel's flag was inspired by the *tallith*, or Jewish prayer shawl; white and blue are the colors of the *tallith*, but they have also come to stand for Israeli nationalist ideals and for the sky. The six-pointed shield, or Star of David, is a traditional Jewish symbol.

MEXICO'S DIAS DE LOS MUERTOS

This annual national holiday begins in Mexico on the evening of October 31 and continues through November 2. Despite its ominous name, Dias de los Muertos (Days of the Dead) is a happy celebration for everyone in the family. Chocolates, sugar skulls, and delicious pastries are sold in the bakeries and *tianguis,* or open-air markets, and fill the air with their sweet scents. Papier-mâché *mascaras,* or masks, are worn; puppets are made; and flowers and *novios* (hearts) are reminders of loved ones.

Dias de los Muertos is not so different from another spirit-filled end-of-October holiday, Halloween. Dias de los Muertos activities can enrich and complement your children's traditional Halloween experiences.

South of the Border Bulletin Board

This unit's bulletin board can act as a scrapbook of activities. As the children finish each project, place the results on the board and display them until the unit has been completed. This will allow the children to anticipate where their artwork will be hung, and to see their creations displayed in a "gallery." At the end of the unit, the children may take all of their work home.

Materials: White poster board, 12" x 18" pieces of construction paper (green, white, and red), tape, nontoxic glue

Directions: From left to right, glue one green, one white, and one red piece of construction paper to the poster board. These colors (in this order) represent the colors of the Mexican flag. As children finish making their *BodyArt* flowers, hearts, and suitcases, tape them on the board for the duration of the unit.

Option: Add travel brochures about Mexico and crepe paper streamers for an additional festive touch!

Say Olé Suitcase

This creative project enables each child to have his or her own adventure-accompanying suitcase!

Materials: Suitcase reproducible (p. 70), scissors, crayons, Velcro, tagboard, crayons, marker, stapler and staples, self-adhesive stickers (optional), masking tape

Directions: Copy, cut out, and color the suitcase reproducible. Fold along the broken line. Add self-adhesive stickers for extra appeal. Next, trace the child's hand (fingers tight together) onto a piece of tagboard. Cut out the paper hand and make a second, identical hand using the first one as a guide. Staple the heels of the paper hands together. Add two small squares of Velcro to each of the middle fingers. One square on each finger should be soft and fuzzy, the other sandpapery. Make sure the two fingers' squares are mirror images of one another. Then slip the paper fingers through the suitcase handle and press the Velcro pieces together to close.

To display the suitcases on the bulletin board, use a small circle of masking tape on the back of one paper palm to adhere the suitcase to the bulletin board.

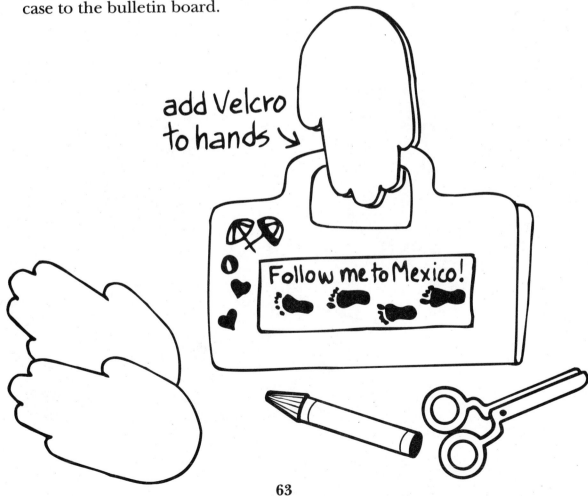

Hanging Novio

Novios, or hearts, are gestures of affection that pay tribute to loved ones—past and present—during Dias de los Muertos family celebrations.

Materials: Nontoxic, pink tempera paint (combine 2 parts white with 1 part red); hole punch; yarn; marker (optional); scissors; shallow paint tray; white poster board; masking tape

Directions: Ask each child to dip one hand (palm side down) into a tray of pink tempera. Have the child make two imprints on the poster board with fingers tightly together, angling the prints so that the fingers of the two hands touch and the palms extend outward.

When the paint has dried, cut out the *novio* from the poster board. Punch a hole in the top portion and loop a 12" piece of yarn through the hole. Tie the yarn into a knot. If you like, use a marker to add names of the child's loved ones in the center of the heart. Display *novios* on the bulletin board by pressing a rolled piece of masking tape to the back. Let the children take home their hearts at the end of the unit.

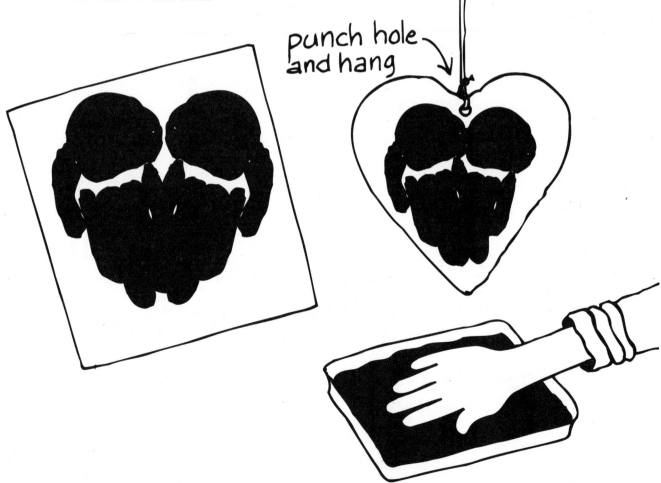

punch hole and hang

Sun and Cloud Flowers

Flowers are an important part of Dias de los Muertos celebrations. *Zempasuchitls* (similar to marigolds—they look like suns) and white blossoms called "clouds" are carried by families on their way to pay their respects to loved ones who have passed on.

Materials: Green and white construction paper; long green pipe cleaners; scissors; yellow and white nontoxic, washable tempera paint; shallow paint trays; tape

Directions: To make *zempasuchitls,* ask each child to dip one hand (palm side down) into a shallow tray of yellow paint. Have the child make three imprints in a row, thumbs and pinkies touching, on white construction paper. When dry, cut out all three paper hands, making sure that the thumbs and pinky fingers are still connected. Roll the paper hands into a horn with fingers extending upward. Pinch and twist the heel sections. Add a stem to the flower by wrapping a pipe cleaner tightly around the twisted heel portion twice and letting the remainder extend straight down. Tape the flowers to the "South of the Border" bulletin board for children to enjoy.

To make "cloud" flowers, repeat the process for *zempasuchitls,* but use white paint and make palm prints on green construction paper.

roll hands, twist, and add pipe cleaner

Mexico Finger Plays and Movement Songs

Sweethearts

(to the tune of "Twinkle, Twinkle, Little Star")

Twinkle, twinkle, hearts are bright,
Shining love through day and night.
Through our laughter and our tears
We remember all the years.

On this very special day,
There's one thing we want to say.
Paper sweethearts we give to you
To tell about our love so true.

Let's Go to Mexico!

(Encourage the children to act out what is being said.)

First, we pack our hat, hat, hat.
Then we pack our shirt, shirt, shirt.
And we pack our pants, pants, pants
So we can dance, dance, dance.

Then we brush our teeth, teeth,
   teeth,
And we wash our face, face, face,
And we comb our hair, hair, hair,
We wish we were there, there, there!

We feed all of our dogs, dogs, dogs.
We feed all of our cats, cats, cats.
We feed all of our fish, fish, fish
And make a wish, wish, wish.

Now we're ready to start, start, start
On our way to fun, fun, fun.
We're ready to go, go, go
To Mexico, co, co!

Moon Dancing

(to the tune of "Ring Around the Rosie"—this humorous version brings to mind special family occasions when children may stay outside late at night)

Let's dance in the moonlight,
We'll laugh and shout all night.
Oh, no!
Mom calls!
We all go home.

Mexico Read-Alouds

Fiction

Ada, Alma Flor. *The Gold Coin.* New York: Atheneum, 1991.

A Central American tale that tells about a thief named Juan, who decides to steal an old woman's golden coin. Juan is thwarted when both coin and old woman disappear, but his efforts to find them take him on a journey that changes his life forever.

Angeles, Maria. *Una Tortilla Para Emilia.* Littleton, Mass.: Sundance, 1993.

Though this book is written in Spanish, you'll be able to understand the story through the pictures if you don't speak Spanish. Emilia, a young girl from a contemporary Mexican-American family, is celebrating her birthday. As more and more young guests arrive, gifts and food are presented, but no tortilla!

Avalos, Cecilia. *The Sombrero of Luis Lucero.* Littleton, Mass.: Sundance, 1993.

More than anything, Luis wants a sombrero like his father's, uncle's, and grandfather's. His mother tells him to go to the wishing shrine, but Luis discovers that the wishing business requires lots of patience!

Hayes, Joe. *Antonio's Lucky Day.* New York: Scholastic, 1993.

This Big Book folktale from Mexico tells the story of a poor farmer's son who learns that daydreaming doesn't put food on the table.

Johnson, Tony. *I'm Gonna Tell Mama I Want an Iguana.* New York: Putnam's, 1990.

This collection of short poems will tickle every funny bone!

Lewis, Thomas. *Hill of Fire.* New York: Harper and Row, 1971.

Be careful what you wish for—it might just happen! A farmer is not happy because nothing ever happens in the village. When a volcano erupts, he learns that there are worse things than being bored!

Schoberle, Cecile. *Esmeralda and the Pet Parade.* New York: Simon & Schuster, 1990.

Juan's pet goat Esmeralde is always getting into trouble, and the results will make young children laugh. Wood block pictures give a feeling of Mexican art and the countryside.

Nonfiction

Cribb, Joe. *Money.* New York: Knopf, 1990.

If reading *The Gold Coin* (see above) sparks an interest in currency among children, this book is a great follow-up. The photos are very realistic; a great reference book for your library.

Wolf, Bernard. *Beneath the Stone.* New York: Orchard, 1994.

This Mexican Zapotec tale features high-quality photographs that give young children a realistic notion of life in an Hispanic community.

Mexico Snacktime

Melting Marshmallow Skulls

Hot chocolate is a traditional festive drink during Dias de los Muertos. When marshmallow "skulls" are added, it's bound to be special! Make skulls by gently pushing chocolate morsels into large marshmallows for eyes and a mouth. Then drop into hot chocolate and watch the skulls disappear!

Mexico Game

Beanbag Toss in the Graveyard

In addition to having fun, here's a chance for children to practice using large motor skills as well as eye-hand coordination.

Materials: Beanbag, six empty coffee cans, tombstone reproducible (p. 69), scissors, paper, crayons or markers, glue or tape

Directions: Copy the tombstone reproducible six times, cut out, and decorate. Then glue or tape one tombstone onto the side of each coffee can to create a graveyard. Line up the coffee cans in a row or place them in varying positions of difficulty. Let each child get a chance to toss the beanbag into a coffee can. When a player is successful, he or she gets to toss again.

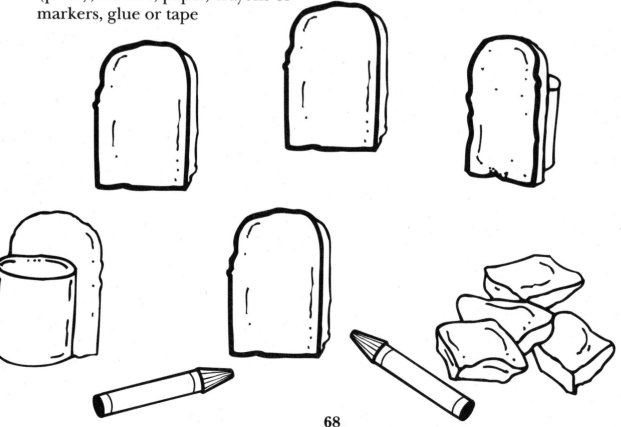

UNITED NATIONS DAY

The United Nations was established on October 24, 1945, to help build peace throughout the world. At that time, 50 nations understood that the world might not survive another World War—the second of which had ended only months before. Since that beginning, more than 100 other nations have joined the U.N., now recognized as a worldwide peacekeeping force.

Even though the concept of global peace is a tough one for young children to understand, the projects in this unit help with their multicultural emphasis. Children need to celebrate holidays, but they also need to celebrate each other's differences. When children learn that each person is unique, appreciation for other people grows. Communication replaces aggression. And as the children grow up, they understand at a deeper level how to master the art of living in a global village.

It's truly exciting to be at this pivotal point in children's development. If you can introduce friendship skills and an appreciation of others in the young, you will make a big difference—not only in their lives but in the lives of those who love them.

Join Hands for Peace Bulletin Board

In this easy-to-make bulletin board, childrens' hands touch as they encircle the United Nations flag. The meaning: We need everybody's help to make the world a "peaceable kingdom." The flag contains all five continents in its center, surrounded by a symbol of peace—a wreath of olive branches.

Materials: Flag reproducible (p. 80); paper; nontoxic glue; white poster board; nontoxic, washable tempera paint (in a variety of skintone colors); shallow paint trays; crayons or markers; scissors

Directions: Copy, color, and cut out the United Nations flag at the end of this unit (continents, olive branches, and longitude and latitude bars are white against a blue field). Glue the flag to the center of the poster board. Fill each paint tray with a different skin-tone color. Ask each child to dip his or her hand (palm side down), one at a time, into a tray and make an imprint. Have children continue making palm prints, making a circle of prints as big as possible without overlapping the bulletin board title. Each print should touch the palm of the print before.

Kristin's Necklace

People in every culture find ways to call attention to and beautify various parts of the body by wearing jewelry. Have fun with this *BodyArt* necklace, whose idea came from a child!

Materials: Construction paper (various colors) or Fun Foam (available in craft stores or from Western Trimming Corp., Chatsworth, CA 91311), scissors, hole punch, yarn, pencil or marker

Directions: Trace the child's fingers onto a piece of Fun Foam or construction paper. Repeat several times for necklace ornaments. Cut out the foam or paper fingers and punch a hole in the top portion of each. Thread a 24" piece of yarn through the holes, with the rounded portion of the paper fingers hanging down. Tie the ends of the yarn together, making sure the necklace is big enough to fit comfortably over the child's head.

Options: Use a shorter piece of yarn to make a bracelet. To make earrings, loop a short piece of yarn and a finger ornament around the child's ear.

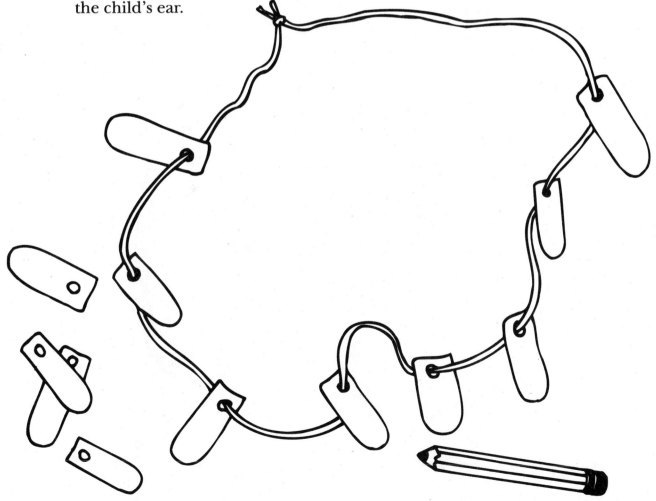

"Hand-y" Tambourines

Cultures throughout the world use music in very special ways: to express feelings, communicate a larger social concern, or carry on traditions and rituals. Playing musical instruments is something shared by everyone in the global community.

Materials: Large paper plates; ribbon or crepe paper (various colors); nontoxic, washable tempera (choice of color); shallow tray; scissors; six medium-sized bells (available from craft stores); stapler and staples; tape; hole punch; nontoxic glue

Directions: Ask the child to dip one hand (palm side down) into a shallow tray of paint. Then have him or her make an imprint in the center of the back of a large paper plate. Repeat on a second paper plate. When both plates are dry, staple the fronts together; tape over staples. Glue ribbon or crepe paper bows around the imprint to decorate. Then punch six holes around the edge of the plates and thread each through with ribbon. (Or add as many holes and ribbons as you'd like.) Add a bell to each piece of yarn and tie closed.

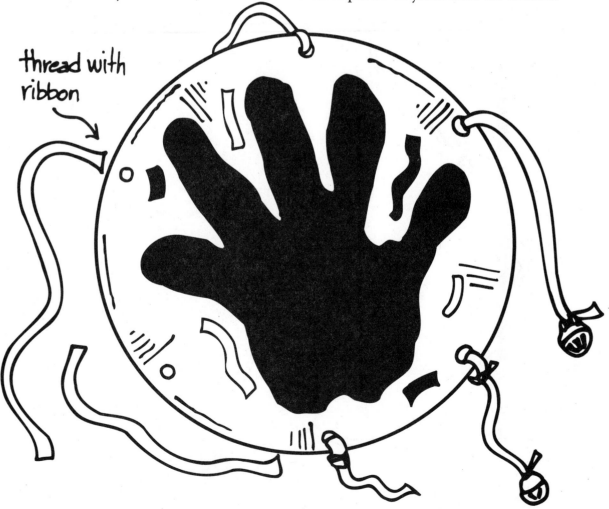

thread with ribbon

Easy Tie Dye Hanging

Although it originated in Africa, tie dying spread to India and other parts of the world. No two designs are alike; just like children, each hanging is unique!

Materials: White coffee filter; painting smocks; disposable plastic gloves; red, green, blue, and yellow food dye; water; scissors; hole punch; yarn; nontoxic, washable tempera; shallow trays; pencil or marker

Directions: Before beginning this activity, have the child put on a smock and gloves and cover the table with a plastic cloth. Then put a small amount of diluted food coloring in each of several trays. Fold a coffee filter lengthwise three or four times. Ask the child to dip the filter into the color of choice, then turn the filter and dip it into another color. When the entire filter is colored, the hanging is ready to open and dry. When completely dry, trace the child's hand (with glove removed) on the filter and cut out. Punch a hole in the top of the filter and loop an 8" piece of yarn through the hole for hanging.

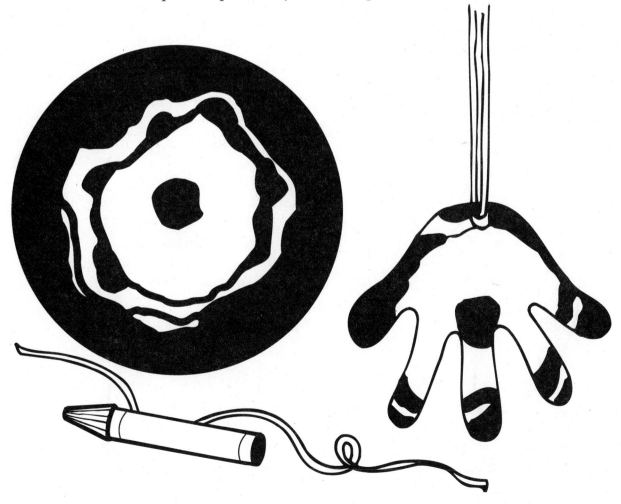

United Nations Day Finger Plays and Movement Songs

Friends Forever!

(to the tune of "Bingo")

I had a friend and he was fun
And Buddy was his name-o.
B-U-D-D-Y,
B-U-D-D-Y,
B-U-D-D-Y
And Buddy was his name-o!

I had a friend and she was nice
And Suzie was her name-o.
S-U-Z-I-E,
S-U-Z-I-E,
S-U-Z-I-E
And Suzie was her name-o!

(Substitute any five-letter names of children in your group.)

Pop Goes the World!

(to the tune of "Pop Goes the Weasel")

All around the whole wide world
There are lots of people living.
They can live most anywhere
And still be our neighbors.

We don't always have to agree,
There are lots of good ideas.
You listen to me and I listen too.
That's the friendly way!

Where Is _____?

(Add child's name to the tune of "Where Is Thumbkin?" To act out this song, sit on the floor in a circle with heads down. As children's names are sung, they raise their heads and everyone greets them. The song is over when each child has had his or her name called.)

Where is _____?
Where is _____?
We miss (him/her),
We miss (him/her).
Oh, there you are sitting,
Glad you are not missing.
We welcome you!
We welcome you!

United Nations Day Read-Alouds

Fiction

Aardema, Verna. *The Crocodile and the Ostrich.* New York: Scholastic, 1993.

This tale from the Akamba of Kenya is available as a Big Book. The story tells how the ostrich got his long neck.

Aardema, Verna. *Rabbit Makes a Monkey of Lion.* New York: Puffin, 1989.

This Swahili tale tells how a small creature made the king of the jungle look as foolish as a monkey.

Aardema, Verna. *Why Mosquitos Buzz in People's Ears.* New York: Dial, 1975.

In this "Reading Rainbow" picture book, Mosquito sets off a chain of events that leads to a jungle disaster. Illustrated by Leo and Diane Dillon. A Caldecott Medal winner.

Agard, John. *The Calypso Alphabet.* Littleton, Mass.: Sundance, 1989.

From the Caribbean Islands comes the alphabet in calypso! Young children will especially enjoy hearing the new sounds as well as looking at the pictures by Jennifer Bert.

Brown, Marcia. *Shadow.* New York: Scribner's, 1982.

This Caldecott Medal winner tells a haunting tale from the French.

Dumbleton, Mike. *Dial-a-Croc.* New York: Orchard, 1991.

Vanessa has a money-making idea and finds a crocodile to help her carry out the plan.

Feelings, Muriel. *Jambo Means Hello.* New York: Dial, 1974.

In this Caldecott Honor book, illustrated by Tom Feelings, young children have the opportunity to learn the Swahili alphabet.

Feelings, Tom. *Soul Looks Back in Wonder.* New York: Dial, 1993.

Thirteen major poets—from Langston Hughes to Walter Dean Myers—offer glimpses of the African-American spirit. A worthy addition to your class library.

Lewin, Hugh. *Jafta's Father.* Minneapolis: Carolrhoda Books, 1983.

Introduce children to the land of bluegum trees, baobabs, and weirs—all of which are explained at the end of this wonderful paperback. Also available by the author: *Jafta and the Wedding, Jafta's Mother,* and *Jafta.*

McDermott, Gerald. *Anansi the Spider.* New York: Holt, 1972.

This Caldecott Honor book tells a tale from the Ashanti of West Africa, in the country of Ghana, where Anansi the spider is a folk hero and lovable trickster. In this story, Anansi is saved from trouble by his sons. The problem is on which son Anansi should bestow his most prized possession.

Peet, Bill. *Eli.* Boston: Houghton Mifflin, 1978.

Eli the lion is a decrepit old cat who lives in the land of Kumbumbazango. He gets into trouble but is saved by a vulture.

Seeger, Pete. *ABIYOYO.* New York: Macmillan, 1986.

The text by singer Pete Seeger tells about a giant and how one boy becomes a hero. The story is based on a South African lullaby and folk story. Illustrated by Michael Hays.

Surat, Michele Maria. *Angel Child, Dragon Child.* New York:Scholastic, 1983.

Mom is far away in Vietnam and cannot comfort Angel Child from the pain of prejudice in America. This "Reading Rainbow" book, illustrated by Vo-Dinh Mai, tells how prejudice destroys hope and self-esteem.

Yashima, Mitsu and Taro. *Plenty to Watch.* New York: Viking, 1954.

On the way home from school there is plenty to watch in the little Japanese village. There's Mr. Blue, the man who dyes yarn and cloth, the hair clippers, and others.

Yashima, Taro. *Crow Boy.* New York: Viking, 1955.

This Caldecott Honor picture book tells about the pain of not belonging that is felt by a little Japanese boy.

Nonfiction

Price, Christine. *Talking Drums of Africa.* New York: Scribner's, 1973.

A lovely nonfiction offering tells poetically about the language of African drums.

United Nations Day Snacktime

Vegetable soup makes a "souper" snack during the United Nations Day unit, because it symbolizes the wonderful mix of the global community.

New-Fangled Vegetable Soup

(serves 8-10)

Large can of vegetable or beef broth
1 small onion, finely chopped

1 cup carrots, diced
1/2 cup celery, diced
2 cups potatoes, diced
Large can of tomato juice or V8 juice (optional)

Put all the ingredients in a large pot with a lid and simmer until the veggies are medium soft (without being mushy). If you prefer to use a crock pot, cook on low for 4 to 6 hours.

United Nations Day Game

Walking Shoes

They say that you really don't know what it's like to be someone else until you've "walked a mile in his or her shoes." Here's a game that gives children a chance to do just that!

Directions: Pile all sorts of shoes (the more sizes the better!) onto the floor. Let each child take a turn walking in any two shoes. (Put a five-minute time limit on play so that everyone gets a chance to wear a pair.) Then play "Follow the Feet" (like "Follow the Leader"), letting the child wearing a certain shoe be the leader. Give everyone a chance to lead.

Note: Don't include shoes with high heels or sharp edges. Also, be sure to have children wear socks with the shoes. If some children don't want to put on other people's shoes, they're still welcome to play the game in their own shoes.